T0269937

GILLY

THE TURBULENT LIFE OF
ROY GILCHRIST

MARK PEEL

First published by Pitch Publishing, 2023

Pitch Publishing
9 Donnington Park,
85 Birdham Road,
Chichester,
West Sussex,
PO20 7AJ
www.pitchpublishing.co.uk
info@pitchpublishing.co.uk

A CIP catalogue record is available for this book
from the British Library.

ISBN 978 1 80150 395 2

Typesetting and origination by Pitch Publishing
Printed and bound in Great Britain by TJ Books, Padstow

Contents

Acknowledgements 5

Introduction. 7

1. 'Country Boy'. 16

2. Blooded in England 35

3. Pummelling Pakistan. 50

4. Beamed into Exile 61

5. Halcyon Days at Middleton 88

6. Ungentlemanly Conduct 109

7. Retribution not Redemption 124

8. Mentoring in India 143

9. 'I don't play in friendlies, even on Sundays'. 160

10. Domestic Strife. 171

11. 'You're some old bloke who can't bowl' 185

12. 'Ches, I'm not going back' 202

Roy Gilchrist 209

Bibliography 216

Index 220

Acknowledgements

I'D LIKE to thank the following for sharing their experiences of Roy Gilchrist: Ed Allen, Steven Barron, Malcolm Blackhurst, Bob Bennett, Peter Boardman, Brian Breese, Mike Buckley, Gerard Cahill, Jim Carnegie, Stephen Chalke, Ed Cooper, Roy Decambre, Chris Debenham, Mike Dunkerley, Ray Davis, Farokh Engineer, Harold Gardner, David Gartside, Cebert Glasgow, Clayton Goodwin, Alan Haigh, Jess Hall, Peter Harvey, Stan Heaton, Jackie Hendriks, Brian Higgin, Michael Holding, Mike Ikin, Stephen Jervis, Alan Lansdale, Vince Lindo, David Lloyd, Malcolm Lorimer, Brian Lymbery, Kevin MacMahon, Doug McLeod, Warwick Milne, Lance Neita, Scott Oliver, Richard Pearce, Glenn Rigby, Gordon Ripley, John Schofield, Jeremy Scholes, Jack Simmons, Edward Slinger, Whit Stennett, Nigel Stockley, Peter Sutcliffe, Frank Taylor, Ivo Tennant, John Turner, Murphy Walwyn, Guy Williams, Neil Williams, Barry Wilson, Cec Wright, Stephen Wright, Gordon Wood.

I would like to extend a special thanks to Roy Gilchrist's partner, Maureen Dixon, his daughter, Jerdaine Dixon, and to Chester Watson who was a fount of information and enlightenment.

I'm also most grateful to Neil Robinson, the Curator of Collections at Lord's and MCC, for all his help, and to Robert

Curphy, the former Archive and Library Manager at Lord's, for his many efforts on my behalf.

I'm also indebted to the staff at Bacup Library, Blackburn-with-Darwen Central Library, Bolton Central Library, City Library, Bradford, Oldham Library and Lifelong Learning Centre, Stoke-on-Trent City Archives, The British Library, the National Library of Jamaica, and The National Library of Scotland.

Finally, I'd like to express my gratitude to my agent Andrew Lownie; to Richard Whitehead for his invaluable copy edit; and to Jane Camillin and Alex Daley at Pitch, along with Duncan Olner, Dean Rockett and Graham Hales for all their efforts on the design, proofing and typeset.

Introduction

ON 14 February 1959, West Indies' highly successful tour of India was in its final stages as they played North Zone at Amritsar. Set 246 to win on a sporting wicket, the home side were floundering against Jamaican fast bowler Roy Gilchrist, who'd pulverised the Indian batsmen throughout the tour with his blistering pace and bristling intimidation.

Undeterred by Gilchrist's aggression, North Zone's captain Swaranjit Singh boasted before the match that he would get the better of him and now, in the second innings, having driven him for four, he swaggered up to him in a provocative show of one-upmanship.

Riled by Singh's taunts, Gilchrist cast all caution aside and began peppering him with a slew of bouncers and beamers (balls aimed directly at the head). After one terrifying delivery that just missed him, Singh appealed to West Indies' captain Gerry Alexander, a friend of his from their time at Cambridge University together, to restrain his fast bowler. Alexander duly obliged, but Gilchrist, in a display of truculent insubordination, ignored his captain's instructions, and when he bowled another beamer the next ball, his fate was sealed. For not only did Alexander order him from the field of play, he also sent him home prematurely, thereby missing the tour to Pakistan that followed. At the age of

24 and on the brink of greatness, Gilchrist never represented his country again.

Much of his volatile personality can be traced to his early hardships in colonial Jamaica. Born into grinding poverty on 28 June 1934, the youngest of 22 children, Gilchrist was brought up on a sugar plantation where his family worked long hours for meagre wages. Inheriting the great West Indian passion for cricket, he spent all his spare time playing the game, his precocious talent bolstered by his fanatical determination to succeed. Although short of stature, he generated great pace through his long, dangling arms, a fast, galloping run-up, a four-yard leap into his delivery stride and a classic side-on action. Having cut a swathe through the island's district competitions, almost by chance he came across William (Bill) Stewart, a leading employer and sponsor, who took him to the capital Kingston, enabling him to play in the Senior Cup, Jamaica's elite cricket competition.

He made an immediate impact and after one season of consistent success, he was chosen for the West Indies tour of England in 1957. Up against superior opponents, the tourists seriously underperformed and were well beaten, but Gilchrist gave notice of his potential, his pace and hostility troubling the cream of the England batting.

That potential rapidly developed when Pakistan visited the West Indies early in 1958. Bowling with sustained hostility on lively wickets, Gilchrist hounded their batsmen throughout the series, not least their talismanic opener Hanif Mohammad. Forced to follow on in the first Test, he saved his country with an epic 337 accumulated over four days, but the constant need to take evasive action against Gilchrist's bouncers increasingly drained his confidence, and he subsequently fell to him five times in succession.

By the end of a rubber which West Indies won convincingly, Gilchrist had cemented his reputation as one of the world's most intimidating bowlers. A summer honing his skills for Middleton on the slow, green wickets of the Central Lancashire League (CLL) further refined his craft, and that winter he and fellow fast bowler Wes Hall wrought havoc in India against opponents who displayed little stomach for the fight. In a series which West Indies won 3-0, Gilchrist took 26 wickets in four Tests at an average of 16, but his combative personality constantly landed him in trouble.

A man of few words off the field, Gilchrist became a man possessed on it with a genuine loathing of batsmen and a desire to inflict maximum damage upon them, including the possibility of killing them. He wrote in his autobiography *Hit Me for Six*, 'I have a reputation for hating batsmen. That comes from being the kind of fellow who really wants to get batsmen out; and that is what every bowler should do – hate the other guy on the field. It was the only way to see them off.'

He continued, 'A beamer is a nasty ball when it comes flying head high at a batsman from my hand. But I have searched the rule books and there is not a word in any of them that says a fellow cannot bowl a fast full-toss at a batsman. Which, after all, is what a beamer is. A batsman *has* got a bat and full-tosses should always get the treatment they deserve.'

Following several breaches of discipline in his previous Tests before the tour of India, Gilchrist was warned about his conduct by manager Berkeley Gaskin, but his headstrong ways soon brought him into conflict with captain Gerry Alexander, a light-skinned Jamaican from a privileged background. Appointed captain to restore discipline in the wake of the disastrous 1957 tour of England, Alexander objected to Gilchrist's contentious use of the beamer and, after the first Test at Bombay, he told him to remove it from his repertoire.

It was an edict that offended Gilchrist's competitive instincts and widened the breach with his captain, who held very different values from his own. In high dudgeon, Gilchrist allowed a minor altercation with team-mate Basil Butcher in practice prior to the second Test at Kanpur to escalate into something more serious when he left the field in defiance of Alexander's command.

Hauled before the tour committee to explain himself, Gilchrist let out his festering resentment against Alexander in an expletive-ridden rant that shocked all who heard it. Consigned to an early departure home, he was only reprieved by a deputation of team-mates who pleaded his case and his own belated apology.

Dropped for the second Test instead, Gilchrist returned in triumph for the rest of the series, but his relationship with his captain remained frayed, so that when he offended once again in the match against North Zone, he paid the ultimate penalty.

His ignominious return home elicited different reactions. The white-dominated West Indies Cricket Board of Control (WICBC) and Jamaica Board of Control both fully supported Alexander, as did many of the leading cricket writers, but amid the general populace the reaction was much more sympathetic to Gilchrist.

Leading the case for the defence was the renowned Trinidadian cricket writer and Marxist intellectual C.L.R. James, who in his quest to end the tradition of a white man captaining the West Indies, was campaigning for Alexander to be replaced by Frank

Worrell. Convinced that the WICBC didn't understand Gilchrist, James suggested that they get in touch with Worrell to extract an apology out of him, since Gilchrist idolised him. The board, however, thought Gilchrist was beyond the pale and refused to select him either for the forthcoming home series against England or the subsequent tour to Australia.

In 1961 they appeared to have a change of heart and invited Gilchrist back to the Caribbean to play in the inter-territorial tournament, from which they would pick the West Indies squad to play against India. Gilchrist duly came but arrived under a cloud following an incident in a league game in England that summer.

Appearing for his club Great Chell against Stone in the North Staffordshire and District League, he'd fallen out with the umpires over allegations of time-wasting and dissent, a display of petulance that earned him a life ban from the league. Although the Jamaica Board of Control professed themselves unconcerned about the ban, their attitude soon changed when the WICBC not only omitted him from the national squad, but also never considered him again.

Embittered by this rebuff, not least because he was never able to give his side of the story, Gilchrist continued to ply his trade in the northern leagues in England for another two decades, continuing to show that same aggression that had marked his Test career, leading to further run-ins with opposing batsmen and umpires. In 1963 a minor tiff with the Australian batsman Lou Laza in an exhibition match turned nasty when they came to blows, and in 1965 Radcliffe, Gilchrist's opponents in the CLL, abandoned the match, complaining of his dangerous bowling.

His plethora of wickets and his box-office appeal made him a valuable, if expensive acquisition, but, once again, violent clashes on the field were matched by trouble off it. After years of testing his wife Novlyn's patience, he was placed on probation for three years at Manchester Crown Court for branding her face with an iron following an argument, and the following year he was imprisoned for breaching his probation order when convicted of assaulting two spectators at a cricket match.

With the coming of middle age, a more mellow Gilchrist continued to enjoy success in the lower leagues, but away from cricket marital problems, financial woes and the onset of Parkinson's disease combined to make life taxing. Alarmed by his plight, he decided to return to Jamaica in 1986, and although he found love with a second family, his homecoming wasn't as happy as it might have been. Increasingly plagued by illness and penury, he cut a poignant figure before dying in July 2001, aged 67.

It goes without saying that Gilchrist had a self-destructive streak and that his loss to Test cricket at 24 was a colossal waste of talent. The more pertinent question that needs to be addressed is whether, with a touch more sensitivity by the authorities, he could have been rehabilitated? Certainly, his mentor Worrell appeared willing to take on this responsibility on becoming captain of West Indies in 1960, but he was denied that opportunity by the WICBC, who hadn't forgiven or forgotten Gilchrist's past misconduct. Whether one attributes their attitude to racial and class prejudice is a moot point, but certainly Gilchrist's career bore the hallmarks of a man whose concept of cricket challenged its traditional image of being a gentlemen's game.

The Victorian ethos of fair play that emanated from the English public schools won allegiance not only from within the nation but also across vast tracts of the Empire. That ethos, so religiously propagated by the Marylebone Cricket Club (MCC) and endorsed by the game's chroniclers, prevailed for most of the 20th century. Yet behind the chivalric ideal there lurked a more hard-headed reality in which the conventions of the game were often breached. From the match-fixers of the 18th century and the gamesmanship of W.G. Grace in the high-Victorian period to the Australian captain Warwick Armstrong in the early 20th century, there were those who took competition to excess.

The most notorious exponent of this ruthless professionalism was the blue-blooded Douglas Jardine, captain of the MCC side to Australia in 1932/33. His tactics of bowling Bodyline – intimidatory bowling at the head and upper body – so riled his opposite number, Bill Woodfull, that he told the MCC manager Pelham Warner during the Adelaide Test that one side was playing cricket and the other wasn't. Jardine justified his tactics by claiming that they in no way contravened the laws of the game and in this he was supported by the MCC committee, who decried the Australian Board of Control's allegations of bad sportsmanship. It was only when Bodyline was employed by West Indies in England the following summer, causing a number of injuries, that MCC finally bowed to Australian pressure and outlawed this dangerous form of bowling.

Despite the banning of Bodyline, its legacy lived on in the form of intimidatory short-pitched bowling. While Bodyline was in a sense a retaliation for the pounding that England had taken from the Australian opening pair of Jack Gregory and Ted McDonald in 1920 and 1921, so Don Bradman, the main target of Bodyline, sought revenge post-war when he let loose his opening pair of Ray Lindwall and Keith Miller on the England batsmen. Even Australian critics baulked at the number of bouncers they bowled and the renowned cricket writer Jack Fingleton, who had played in the Bodyline series, accused Bradman of flouting the spirit of cricket.

With the game becoming more professional and umpires reluctant to apply the law on intimidatory bowling, especially since there was some doubt at what constituted a bouncer, short-pitched bowling intensified in the 1950s, not least in the West Indies where a new generation of fast bowlers was coming to prominence.

Raised in the gladiatorial environment of street cricket which celebrated aggression and one-upmanship, fast bowlers such as Gilchrist were accorded a special status in the popular consciousness. Convinced that intimidation was a legitimate part of their armoury, few pacemen resisted the temptation to bowl short and attempt to establish a psychological hold over the batsmen. In turn a number of batsmen rose to the challenge and dispatched them to all parts, all of which contributed significantly to the brio of West Indies cricket. Here in this raucous setting, heightened by national and racial self-assertion against the colonial system, the cricket bore little resemblance to the musings of Henry Newbolt, Neville Cardus and other guardians of the game's conscience. Taking their lead from England's Fred Trueman, who upset Jamaicans in 1953/54 with his sustained assault on their ageing idol George Headley, or Australia's Lindwall and Miller when they toured the following year, they aimed to bowl as fast as possible, none more so than Gilchrist. With his penchant for bowling bouncers and beamers along with a suspect action, he stretched the game's conventions to breaking point and precipitated a rift with the cricketing establishment.

That rift grew ever wider as West Indies fast bowlers from Wes Hall and Charlie Griffith right through to their revered pace quartets of the 1970s and 1980s increasingly dominated international cricket. While their relentless assault at the batsman's body and the proliferation of serious injuries won them few friends, the latter were conveniently forgetting the times when West Indies themselves had been at the mercy of extreme pace, be it Lindwall and Miller or Dennis Lillee and Jeff Thomson.

When the issue of intimidatory bowling became bound up with other aspects of gamesmanship – be it verbal abuse towards an opponent, dissent towards umpires or ball-tampering – it was time for the game's authorities to step in. The introduction of an international code of conduct, match referees and the Decision Review System have helped restore some order to the game, but the fact that statutory regulations were needed largely undermines the idea that cricket encapsulates a higher morality. It is in this context that the life and career of Roy Gilchrist should be examined.

Chapter 1

'Country Boy'

OF ALL the outposts of the cricketing universe few can match the vibrancy and passion of Jamaica, the third-largest island in the Caribbean, some 90 miles south of Cuba. Yet behind its natural beauty and the cultural vibrancy of its mixed-race population, which has made it a popular holiday resort, there lies a troubled past, the legacy of a malformed social system based on prejudice and oppression. This system can be traced back to the Spanish, who first colonised the island following the arrival of the explorer Christopher Columbus in 1494. They enslaved most of the indigenous Arawak Indians and imported large numbers of African slaves to Jamaica as labourers, a process greatly expanded by the British, who conquered the island from the Spanish in 1655.

It was under British rule that many plantations for sugar, cocoa and coffee were established, built on extensive use of slave labour. In the 18th century the sugar industry flourished, bringing untold wealth to the mother country and the Jamaican planters, although their callous exploitation of the slaves – more than three million Africans were forcibly transported to the British colonies in the Caribbean – provoked numerous slave uprisings, especially in Jamaica in 1765 and 1831.

Despite the abolition of the slave trade in 1807 and the emancipation of slavery in the British Empire in 1834, conditions for migrant black labour remained wretched as the Jamaican sugar industry, facing competition from large estates in Cuba and the Dominican Republic, declined. Their plight, exacerbated by drought, disease and crop failure, inflamed racial tensions, culminating in the Morant Bay Rebellion of 1865, an uprising which was brutally suppressed by Governor Edward John Eyre.

The removal of Eyre and the establishment of direct rule from London brought about the growth of the country's infrastructure, but the island's white elite continued to exercise economic and political power, not least on the plantations which had changed little since emancipation. Detached from the native population through family ties, education and membership of the same exclusive clubs, that elite looked down on the black man as an inferior being – ill-qualified for leadership and responsibility.

It wasn't simply racial divisions that wracked Jamaica. Class divisions were also apparent on the plantations, in the professions and in cricket clubs as a gulf opened up between the educated black middle class and the masses. This continued even after independence in 1962.

In contrast to the privileged lifestyle of the white plantation elite, the majority of Jamaicans continued to suffer from extreme poverty and discrimination manifest in the plethora of strikes during the First World War. During that war, 15,600 West Indians, the majority from Jamaica, enlisted with the British West Indies Regiment, but were still subject to extreme racial discrimination. The 9th Battalion revolted at Taranto in Italy in December 1918. Returning home with a commitment to social and political change, these soldiers found a champion in Marcus

Garvey, the Jamaican-born political activist and black nationalist, who, through his Universal Negro Improvement Association, founded in 1914, helped create a sense of national consciousness and black self-empowerment throughout the Caribbean.

This new sense of working-class solidarity and protest was evident throughout the depressed 1930s when the markets for sugar and bananas collapsed, forcing down wages and creating mass unemployment. The decline in living standards, in addition to peasant unrest with the outdated land-tenure structure and general racism, spawned hunger marches, violent strikes and political protest. In Jamaica, the turbulence led to the emergence of the charismatic Alexander Bustamante as the principal spokesman of the industrial working class and the formation of the left-wing People's National Party, co-founded by Norman Manley. According to his son, Michael Manley, himself a future prime minister of Jamaica, 'This organisation became both the symbol of Jamaica's emergent nationalism, the means through which nationalist energies were directed and the organisation which mobilised the demand for independence.'

The civic and labour unrest across the Caribbean prompted the British government to appoint the Moyne Commission to study conditions there. Its findings led to better wages and a constitution for Jamaica that inaugurated a period of limited government. The first general election under universal adult suffrage was held in December 1944 and the following year Bustamante, leader of the conservative Jamaica Labour Party, took office as the island's first chief minister.

Against a growing climate of unrest, Roy Gilchrist was born on 28 June 1934 at Seaforth, a small, residential town in the parish of St Thomas at the south-east end of the island. Despite its proximity to the capital Kingston, St Thomas is renowned for its mountainous terrain and pristine coastline; it also happens to be the poorest of Jamaica's 14 parishes, blighted by unemployment, poor facilities and illiteracy. Perhaps it is no coincidence that the parish capital, Morant Bay, was the site of the greatest civil unrest in Jamaica's history. One of the largest employers in the area was the Serge Island sugar estate, founded around 1750 by John Garband and named as an island because it was situated between the Negro and Johnson rivers. In December 1937 it became the scene of a bitter labour dispute when cane workers, spurred on by outside agitators, went on strike for higher wages, leading to mass arrests.

It was there that Gilchrist's parents, Charles and Lucy, lived and worked. Little is known about them. Throughout his life Roy was always reticent about his upbringing, even with close friends and family, but it seems likely that Charles Gilchrist met Lucy Davis in Panama, to where many Jamaicans had migrated to work on the construction of the Panama Canal between 1904 and its opening in 1914. In his autobiography, Roy's only reference to his parents were the occasions he took over his father's job on his day off and their subsequent move to another farm on the estate, which meant a long walk to see them. From other sources we learn of two visits to his mother in Jamaica – Christmas 1960 and Christmas 1961 – but that is it. Extra-marital relationships, illegitimacy and large families were extremely common in Jamaica and while there is no cast-iron proof that Gilchrist was illegitimate, it seems likely that many of his siblings were. Mystery surrounds the exact size of his family. Newspapers of the time asserted that he was the youngest of 22 children but others disagree. The Jamaican historian Arnold Bertram wrote that he had 19 siblings; C.L.R. James, who investigated his background, put the number at 21, while Chester Watson, the Jamaica and West Indies fast bowler, was told he was one of 26. Whatever the true number, only two of his siblings are mentioned in his autobiography: John, a successful businessman, and Samuel, who remained on the estate. A sister, Gertrude Gordon, later lived in the USA, but Roy had little contact with her.

With such a large family to tend to in addition to their long hours at work, parental time with the young Roy appears to have been limited. Given his obsession with playing cricket, this might not have bothered him too much in childhood, but growing up without a firm guiding hand had its consequences, not least in the public arena. Throughout his career, Gilchrist depended on father figures such as Bill Stewart, Frank Worrell and Chester Watson to help bring stability to his life. But hard though they tried, they couldn't compensate for his lack of life skills, a problem exacerbated by his father's unwillingness to send him to school, something he later resented. For not only did his lack of education deepen his inferiority complex, it also left him blind to alternative points of view or to subtle nuances of behaviour, leading to arguments developing out of nothing and to rifts in friendships.

Yet whatever the hardships of his formative years – and at least there was always enough to eat – Gilchrist depicted them in rather romantic terms. 'Life was good and life was pretty easy,' he wrote in his autobiography. 'Gilly junior got away with most things because out there and on that estate, everyone thinks, talks and plays cricket and that was one thing I could do really well.' Playing the game all the year round at every conceivable opportunity, Gilchrist teamed up with the Gordon brothers and at dusk after they'd finished, they went along to a nearby bridge to ogle the local girls and engage in some irreverent banter with them. Forming a particularly close relationship with Albert Gordon, Gilchrist thought him a wonderfully gifted cricketer who could have gone far in the game had he displayed the necessary commitment.

Another cricketing mate was Hedley Reid, a useful wicketkeeper, who worked in the estate rum shop; later he became a neighbour of Gilchrist's in Manchester, by which time Reid was no longer playing cricket.

Ever since cricket was introduced to Jamaica in the middle of the 19th century as a leisure pursuit by British officers, it remained part of the imperial order. Blacks were encouraged to take it up as a means of deterring them from rebellious activity, but only in an inferior capacity as bowlers and fielders. All power remained with the white elite through their membership of the most exclusive clubs, the captaincy of the island XI and their control of the Jamaica Cricket Board. Yet following in the footsteps of the charismatic Trinidad and West Indies all-rounder Learie Constantine, whose exploits in the 1920s and 1930s inspired black West Indian cricketers, Jamaica found a true hero in George Headley. Born in Panama to West Indian parents in 1909 – his father had moved there as a construction worker on the Panama Canal – Headley overcame poverty and prejudice to become one of the greatest players of all time. Making his debut for West Indies in 1930, he quickly established himself as a batsman of the highest class who challenged the old stereotype that only whites could bat at the top of the order. In addition to his prodigious run-scoring that led to him being nicknamed the 'black Bradman', his tactical acumen and dignified personality in the face of injustice made him ideally qualified to captain his country. Although that honour eluded him, aside from one Test against England in 1948, he helped give a voice to the new mood of black consciousness throughout the cricket-playing Caribbean, where a new generation of black cricketers, led by the Barbadian trio of Everton Weekes, Frank Worrell and Clyde Walcott, had come to the fore.

Despite Jamaica being the largest of the cricketing islands in the Caribbean and the leading player in the evolution of West Indian nationalism, it assumed a secondary role in the development of its cricket. Located some 1,500 miles from Barbados and the other cricketing centres in the eastern Caribbean, Jamaica was absent from the inter-territorial contests that originated in the 1890s and she didn't play regular first-class cricket until 1964. Her peripheral status saw her patronised by Barbados, Trinidad and British Guiana, which in turn bred a resentment complex. According to Worrell, a Barbadian who moved to Jamaica, 'Few Jamaicans can bear even the mildest exposure of their weaknesses. Even fewer seem willing to make themselves unpopular by drawing attention to the shortcomings of their fellow countrymen … even when they are willing to concede they exist. Instead, they dwell on the failure of non-Jamaicans.'

In a community such as Jamaica, where nearly everyone embraced cricket, makeshift games sprang up all over the island: in fields, in the street or on the beach with bats made of coconut branches, balls of adaptable fruit encased in cloth and stumps of wood or sugar cane. To the accompaniment of large, vociferous crowds and rapturous music, these games bristled with aggression, pride of place going to those who batted with panache and bowled with fire. And it was each man for himself, since local rules dictated that the only way one got to bat was to dismiss the batsman, which, in terms of catches, meant the fielder rather than the bowler. With no umpires and no lbws allowing batsmen to stand in front of their stumps, many a bowler developed a callous streak by bowling as fast as they could in order to hurt those batsmen who placed their legs in the way of the target.

Whether it was their athleticism, the hard pitches in the Caribbean, or the opportunity to release pent-up tension about their lot in society, the West Indies have produced a long list of fast bowlers, all black, dating back to George John pre-1914 and continuing with George Francis, Learie Constantine, Herman Griffith, Manny Martindale and Leslie Hylton. Now, after an absence of real pace in the post-war era, a new generation led by Gilchrist, Wes Hall, Lester King, Charlie Griffith and Chester Watson was fast emerging.

Like Hall, and, later, Michael Holding, Gilchrist didn't begin life as a quick bowler. He used to bowl spin, taking a quiet pride in the ability to 'turn them a bit', and was encouraged to become an off-spinner by Jack Mercer, the Glamorgan and Northamptonshire cricketer, who coached in the sugar estates in Jamaica. In the nets, however, he liked to bowl fast and the more he experimented the more he discovered a raw talent. Encouraged by the foreman of his estate, he began to dream big. He was greatly helped in his endeavours by Tom 'Godfather' Smellie, a popular sportsman from Morant Bay. Smellie, a fast bowler himself, not only provided plenty of support and technical expertise, he also drove him hard. Although a stockily built 5ft 7in and eight stone in weight, hardly the prototype physique of a fast bowler, Gilchrist developed great strength of shoulder, elbow and calf by weightlifting at a local club, and gained propulsion from a speedy, rhythmic approach to the wicket before unwinding with a huge leap in his delivery stride and an explosive whirl of his arms. Asked why he left the ground, Gilchrist would respond,

'Power, I was short, and I had to get as high as possible. I was small, so I had to throw everything into it.'

Intimidation was nothing new in a fast bowler but Gilchrist bore hostility towards the batsman more than most in his fanatical determination to succeed. 'I play to win,' he used to say. 'I don't like losing. I don't think there is any such thing as a good loser. Everyone wants to win.' While most fast bowlers derived little satisfaction from hurting a batsman, especially blows to the head, Gilchrist wasn't burdened by such guilt, figuring that any emotion on his part might build up the batsman's confidence. He wrote, 'When I was young, very young to the game of cricket, I bowled the only way I knew – *flat out*. And there were those who felt that I was not being fair because I was bowling flat out at batsmen who were young. I was told firmly that this would not do.

'It did not seem to matter that I was young too. "Why," I asked them, smiling and trying to be fair, "does it make a difference when I am young and the batsman is young and we are both trying to play the game as we think right?"'

Having made his mark with the Seaforth community team, Gilchrist came to the notice of the wider public when opening the bowling for Serge Island in the Crum Ewing sugar estates competition. Although the Jamaica Cricket Board was negligent about promoting the game in the rural areas, the interest taken by the sugar estates did help provide opportunities for the plantation poor to play with the more fortunate on well-appointed grounds in front of passionate crowds. The 1950s was the heyday of sugar estate cricket. They all had a loyal body of support that added to the sense of occasion at these keenly fought games and Serge Island, with its quaint, rustic ground nestled in a bend of the Johnson River, was no exception. Given the high standard of the cricket, sugar estates went in search of talented cricketers and with people attracted by the better-paid jobs and higher status on the estates, there was no shortage of recruits.

In 1953 Gilchrist enhanced his profile by taking 6-13 against Innswood, who were dismissed for 33, and 5-26 against Gray's Inn Central. The next year, Serge Island won the Wright and Holgate trophies and Gilchrist topped the bowling averages in three tournaments. Ed Allen, later a good friend in Manchester, recalls playing for the neighbouring community of Beacon Hill at Serge Island and being aware of all the local talk about this little man who bowled really fast. Facing up to Gilchrist with the crowd roaring encouragement as he bounded in on his long run, Allen didn't see the ball. Not only was he lightning fast, he later recollected, he also exuded menace.

Gilchrist also represented the parish of St Thomas in the inter-parish Nethersole Cup and although he was dropped after his first match against Portland he was soon back in favour, cementing his place with 7-3 against the St Thomas Police, who were all out for 13. Describing that game as one of his greatest, he was later to write that 'I don't think I've ever done anything better than that. The thrill of that performance still lingers on.'

In late 1954 Gilchrist left St Thomas for the parish of St James, located on the north-west end of the island. For a time, he worked for his brother John, who gravitated from his job as a cabinet maker on the Serge Island estate to running two hairdressing salons and a rum bar in the tourist resort of Montego Bay, the capital of St James. Thinking that Gilchrist might have a future in barbering, John took him in and taught him the essentials, but although Gilchrist quite enjoyed the work and living with his brother and his wife, an ex-nurse, his commitments in the salon restricted his opportunities to play cricket. He thus gave up hairdressing and returned to the plantations.

One of the sugar estates he worked on was the Rose Hall Estate, some ten miles from Montego Bay, and former home to the notorious Annie Palmer, a society beauty whose tyrannical treatment of her slaves led to her killing in a slave uprising in 1831. Out of curiosity, Gilchrist and his workmates used to visit the dilapidated Georgian mansion, formerly one of Jamaica's great plantation houses, where she lived and which was never occupied again following her strangulation. He wrote, 'It always had us frightened, but we still went there and looked and explored. It made us feel somehow big and famous, living on an estate where a celebrity like Alice [sic] Palmer had lived and died.'

From Rose Hall, Gilchrist drifted in and out of work, including a brief spell at the Longpond Estate in the parish of Trelawny, before getting a job in a machine shop on the neighbouring Vale Royal Estate. It was while playing for Longpond that he first made an impression on Jackie Hendriks, later the Jamaica and West Indies wicketkeeper, and his team of party-loving friends in a 'curry goat' match. This type of game was a well-established Jamaican tradition whereby rural clubs would play host to their city counterparts in weekend friendlies, in which the local hospitality, featuring a sumptuous goat-curry lunch and raucous music, was as important as the cricket. Not on this occasion. Bowling on a concrete wicket covered by a decaying piece of matting, Gilchrist was so frighteningly fast that the opposition had little stomach for the fight and were shot out cheaply.

Another to be awestruck by his intimidating pace and his aggression towards batsmen was all-rounder Whit Stennett, later a good friend in Manchester, when playing for St Anne's Bay against Trelawny. He found it curiously exciting watching him run up to the wicket and then his huge leap in his delivery stride. 'I was rather amazed that a man who bowled with such hostility and venom would be so quiet, almost shy to a point,' recalled Stennett. 'My opening gambit to him was, "Paceman, do you touch the iron?" meaning did he do weight training. He did and he felt that I had the ability to make myself into a useful medium-pacer with a deadly yorker. It was quite flattering.'

Playing for St James parish in 1955, Gilchrist immediately made his name in the Hart Cup competition. He also impressed the legendary George Headley, who'd returned to Jamaica that year as national coach with a remit to develop the game in rural areas. On seeing Gilchrist bowl for the first time, he was amazed how such a slight physique could generate such speed. He invited him to his coaching sessions, where he also came under the tuition of Headley's childhood friend Dickie Fuller, a genial giant of a man who played one Test against England in 1935. Gilchrist was also selected to play for a combined parish side under Headley's leadership against the touring Australians, but persistent rain deprived him of his first taste of the big time, much to his disappointment. 'This was a real stunning blow for me,' he wrote, 'for I was making a bit of a name for myself and I had hoped to enhance it further in the game with the Aussies.'

He did, however, enjoy a major piece of good fortune when Kingston businessman Bill Stewart, a man Gilchrist alluded to as his 'fairy godfather', took his private team, the Musketeers, to the Vale Royal Estate, Trelawny, for a holiday game. Stewart, a light-skinned manager of a commercial establishment on the Lascelles Wharf, dealing with ships and goods, was a man of trust, compassion and good judgement. Having noted Gilchrist's prodigious talent and feeling it was being wasted, he invited him to the capital Kingston, a bustling, overcrowded city, and offered him a job and good-class cricket. Gilchrist immediately accepted and Stewart went out of his way to look after him when he arrived in the city. Appreciating that he would like to live on his own, Stewart found him a flat, bought him furniture and helped him set up home. He gave him a job as a forklift operator, teaching him how to drive one of the small engines which carried goods up and down the wharf and in the warehouses. It wasn't a demanding job but Gilchrist mastered it and proved himself to be a willing worker. Stewart certainly didn't think him a paragon of virtue but Gilchrist, he said, would do anything he told him to do and would never resort to anything which he thought would offend him. 'I love Gilchrist as a son,' he later told C.L.R. James, 'almost as much as my own son.' They were feelings amply reciprocated. Placing Stewart on a pedestal with his brother John, he wrote, 'They took hold of that little fellow called "Gilly" – that's what they call me – and changed him into a man. They changed him from a little boy with dreams to a man who saw his dreams coming true.'

Gilchrist enjoyed the job nearly as much as playing for Stewart's Musketeers, one of the strongest weekend sides on the island, which included future Test opener Easton McMorris and Colin and Neville Bonitto, all of whom represented Jamaica. In one game he came across Frank Worrell, one of the West Indies' finest batsmen, for the first time. Worrell sat in a room in the pavilion reading a book on philosophy, oblivious to the mayhem Gilchrist was causing in the middle. Eventually he asked a team-mate, 'What's going on?', whereupon he was told that Gilchrist was terrifying everyone with his pace. Worrell put on his pads and an old sunhat, marched out and scored 84 at a run a minute. On his return, he removed his pads and said, 'See boys, Mr Gilchrist can be hit.'

Gilchrist's coming to Kingston in his attempt to play first-class cricket was a rarity in those days, since Jamaica's highly polarised society offered few opportunities to those emanating from the provinces. Most players representing the island in inter-colonial cricket graduated through the elite schools such as Kingston College, Wolmer's and Jamaica College and exclusive clubs such as Kingston, Melbourne and Kensington. With Stewart's help, Gilchrist was signed up by Wembley, a club with a broader social intake than most, but this didn't stop him being referred to as 'country boy' or subjected to racist asides. In those days, he kept his own company, rarely answering back and causing little trouble to his captain Colin Bonitto, but the insults left him sensitive to slights – real or imaginary – thereafter and enhanced his suspicion that his plantation background earned him a harsher disciplinary record than was proportionate.

Wembley was one of 12 clubs that participated in the Senior Cup, Jamaica's leading cricket tournament, each match played over two Saturdays. Before their opening game in March 1956 they claimed that they had unearthed a sensational fast bowler in Gilchrist, who, they predicted, would make an imposing first appearance. Their words proved uncannily accurate, since after Gilchrist's 6-60 against that season's champions, Kingston, he was described by the island's leading newspaper, the *Jamaica Gleaner*, as the best prospect seen in the competition for a very long time and a future West Indian fast bowler in the making. 'Displaying an easy run, and good action, Gilchrist bowled accurately and untiringly from both ends, and had most of the Kingston batsmen groping in the dark.'

A month later he went one better with seven wickets against the University of West Indies, who, needing only 64 for victory, were bowled out for 41, their batsmen beaten for sheer pace.

He was equally aggressive in his 7-50 against Garrison, helping Wembley to a nine-run victory. On one occasion the ball took the edge of the bat, flew past the slips and nearly went for six. No wonder the soldiers thought seriously of retreat and taking evasive action in the general direction of square leg. 'This is the second time this season that Wembley has scored fewer than 109 runs and won, and on both occasions, they were saved by the hostile fast bowling of this mild and peaceful fast bowler,' wrote Sydney 'Foggy' Burrowes in *Public Opinion*, a nationalist Jamaican tabloid. 'This wild Bill Elliott of the cricket field seems to be an admirable marksman and the 14 wickets he took in both these games were all bowled and lbw.

'Gilchrist played cricket in the Country parts up to last year without attracting undue attention, but his opportune arrival in the Corporate Area makes him a certainty for the Corporate Area and St Catherine team to go to Antigua.'

Not every batsman fell prey to his pace. The following week West Indies batsman Collie Smith hit a century off him, exposing his lack of variety and genuine surprise that any batsman should gain the upper hand over him.

Gilchrist's 26 wickets at 11.80 in the Senior Cup not only placed him third in the competition's bowling averages, it helped win him a place on the Jamaican Colts' tour to Antigua. There they played against both the Combined Windward-Leeward Islands Colts and British Guiana Colts, and although he took only one wicket, his pace gained the attention of his opponents.

Chosen for the Jamaica trials, Gilchrist was again among the wickets, impressing Vince Lindo, a talented all-rounder with the Garrison club. He recalled his deceptive action, especially the complete circle with his arms before delivery, making it harder for batsmen to pick up the line and length of the ball, and his prodigious appetite. In one game in which Gilchrist was playing, he ate all the tea, leaving none for the other players. 'Roy had a very good appetite and you didn't argue,' Lindo commented.

Gilchrist's exploits won him selection for Jamaica in the four-way inter-colonial held at Georgetown, British Guiana. Consigned to field first against a very strong Guyanese batting line-up on a placid Bourda Oval wicket, Gilchrist still managed to turn heads on the opening morning by working up real pace. He soon dismissed Glendon Gibbs and had his moments against West Indies opener Bruce Pairaudeau and promising tyro Rohan Kanhai, but in perfect batting conditions the pair stood firm and gradually took control. Both scored centuries and although Gilchrist eventually dismissed Pairaudeau and had Clyde Walcott lbw for 26, there was no respite, since two promising newcomers, Basil Butcher and Joe Solomon, both scored centuries, adding an unbeaten 281 in their side's 601/5 declared.

Butcher, playing against Gilchrist for only the second time, later recalled that he was the fastest bowler he ever saw. 'So when Statham and those [English] guys were bowling, they weren't bowling at any pace to scare anybody.

'Gilly was a serious cricketer. I remember I pushed this ball past Gilly at Bourda, and Gilly took off and saved one run. Gilly and Lance Gibbs had the same competitive mentality.'

He finished with 3-129 and won the admiration of others besides his captain Allan Rae, the former West Indies opening batsman. Seymour Coppin, the sports editor of the *Barbados Advocate*, tipped him as the leading West Indies fast bowler for the 1957 tour to England, and the Trinidad manager Harold Burnett, himself a former first-class cricketer, thought his bowling the fastest seen in the Caribbean since Manny Martindale in the 1930s. It was a view with which the former West Indies all-rounder Ben Sealey concurred. He called Gilchrist the most sensational pace-bowling discovery in the previous 20 years, rating him much more astute than any other West Indian fast bowler in the post-war era. If the selectors failed to pick him for the forthcoming tour of England, he averred, they would be guilty of an 'unpardonable sin'.

Philip Thomson, *The Cricketer*'s special correspondent in the West Indies, alerted British readers to his great promise. 'Playing in first-class Intercolonial cricket for the first time, the 20-year-old youth with the long run showed that he had the pace to get the ball to lift even on the docile Bourda wicket. … A small man he is nevertheless square of shoulder, can bowl long spells, and is at the moment the most talked of-cricketer in the islands.'

These accolades delighted 'Strebor' Roberts, the sports editor of the *Daily Gleaner*, but warned Gilchrist that he would need to work harder if he was to fully realise his potential.

Gilchrist's raw pace attracted the interest of the West Indies selectors, who picked him for the two trial games in Trinidad that would help determine their team to tour England. Before the departure of the Jamaican players, in a practice on some makeshift concrete wickets at Kingston Racecourse, Jackie Hendriks recalls guiding a well-pitched-up ball from Gilchrist through the covers, much to the approval of the large crowd, but their cheers infuriated

Gilchrist, who then bowled a really quick ball that hit a little boy in the crowd yards behind the wicket.

At practice at the Queen's Park Oval, Port-of-Spain, he was the biggest attraction. Making the ball rear nastily against several Guyanese batsmen, he persuaded their captain Clyde Walcott to withdraw them for their own safety and when Walcott batted, he opted for an all-spin attack. In the two trials, played on the flattest of surfaces, Gilchrist was the most successful fast bowler with eight wickets, including the prized dismissal of Walcott in the first game and that of Everton Weekes in the second. (He also dislocated wicketkeeper Hendriks's finger.) Although prone to spells of waywardness, it was a performance good enough to win him a berth on the boat to England, along with five other Jamaicans. One local writer enthused, 'It was again encouraging to see a ring of fieldsmen around and behind the wicket when a West Indian was bowling in a first-class match,' while Strebor Roberts wrote, 'Roy Gilchrist's rapid rise to the top is another Ramadhin-Valentine story. To have made a West Indies team in one season of Senior Cup cricket is a remarkable achievement.'

While delighted with his inclusion, Gilchrist was disconcerted by the exclusion of Leeward Islands wicketkeeper John Reid, which he attributed to the arbitrary manner in which the WICBC ran the game. Throughout its history West Indies cricket had been bedevilled by inter-island rivalries which helped account for some flawed selections, not least during the mid-1950s over the position of wicketkeeper when Alfie Binns, Clifford McWatt and Clairmonte Depeiaza were all tried but found wanting.

According to Gilchrist, Reid's flawless exhibition during the trial game made the other 'keepers look like 'stoppers' and he ascribed his omission to the fact that he played for the lowly

Leeward Islands. Equally controversial was the inclusion of the Cambridge-educated Gerry Alexander, subsequently to be Gilchrist's nemesis, especially since he'd yet to play for Jamaica. Comparing his ability to Reid, Gilchrist thought he looked like a novice whose selection owed much to his contacts, although he subsequently credited him with a tremendous improvement.

Before departure Jamaica hosted the Duke of Norfolk's touring side, which comprised England players such as Willie Watson and Tom Graveney and the former West Indies batsman Roy Marshall. Desperate to dismiss Marshall, whom he highly rated, Gilchrist saw wicketkeeper Alexander, making his debut for Jamaica, drop him off his first ball, much to his frustration. In that first game, in which he took 5-110 in the first innings, he broke Hampshire wicketkeeper David Blake's wrist and although he did little thereafter in the three-match series, the tourists were impressed enough by his hostility to warn their team-mates back home about the hurricane fast approaching.

Chapter 2

Blooded in England

THE WEST Indian side that journeyed to England in April
1957 set sail on a high tide of optimism. While the nucleus of
the victorious side of 1950 – Weekes, Worrell, Walcott, Sonny
Ramadhin and Alf Valentine – was still intact, it was boosted
by promising youngsters such as Gary Sobers, Collie Smith and
Rohan Kanhai. Yet the decision to reappoint John Goddard as
captain reflected all too starkly the prejudices and divisions that
blighted West Indian cricket, especially the principle that the
captain should be a white man. Learie Constantine spoke for
many with his conviction that white West Indians couldn't fuel
the same intensity of purpose as their black compatriots and a
black captain was needed to foster solidarity.

Goddard, a wealthy white Barbadian, was no mean cricketer
and had won plaudits for leading West Indies to victory in
England in 1950, but the personal acclaim had irked many of his
team-mates who thought he had leaned greatly on their advice.
Their refusal to cooperate with him helped foment division on the
West Indies tour to Australia in 1951/52, where they lost 4-1 to
Lindsay Hassett's side. Goddard publicly criticised the WICBC
for the tour itinerary, which led to his omission from the Test side

for the next four years as the captaincy passed to his rival Jeffrey Stollmeyer, a wealthy Trinidadian of Anglo-German descent.

Stollmeyer was a stylish opener and respected captain who led his country until 1955 before injury and island rivalries brought about his premature retirement. His natural successor was Frank Worrell, his vice-captain against England in 1953/54, but Worrell was a man of strong convictions and, tiring of Barbados' rigid class system, left for Jamaica in 1947, a move that alienated many. It was probably his tendency to speak out that led to his ousting as Stollmeyer's deputy against Australia the following year in favour of the white Barbadian all-rounder Denis Atkinson, a decision which Stollmeyer called preposterous. The fact that it occurred months after the ill-fated MCC tour when the white West Indian establishment had pleaded with Hutton's men to beat their own team in order to impede the cause of black rule across the Caribbean only added fuel to the fire.

Having captained West Indies in three of the five Tests against Australia in place of the injured Stollmeyer, a series they lost 3-0, Atkinson, whose double century helped save the fourth Test, was then appointed captain of the 1955/56 tour to New Zealand. The selectors also recalled Goddard as player-manager and against mediocre opposition he impressed in his side's 3-1 win. But reappointing him as captain for the 1957 England tour over both Stollmeyer, now restored to full fitness, and Worrell seemed a retrograde move. His limitations as a tactician and a player, combined with his growing remoteness as the tour progressed, was one major cause of a touring party that was riddled with dissension from the outset.

Aside from traditional island rivalries and the gulf between the white amateurs and the rest of the party – on the voyage over the whites went cabin class while the black professionals were in steerage – the decision to appoint joint managers proved a major blunder, especially since Tom Peirce, a former captain of Barbados, and Cecil de Caires, a Guyanese hockey player, had different priorities.

Even before the team's arrival, Gilchrist's inclusion was the cause of press comment. 'Take a look at Gilchrist, the truck driver they call the Black Flash,' wrote Brian Chapman in the *Daily Mirror.* 'No Adonis at first sight!'

'He's a scraggy five-foot seven and nine-stone nine.

'Yes, Roy is a character all right. He is the youngest of 22 children who between them could stage a complete Sons and Daughters match – no doubt with Father and Mother umpiring. He has met life the tough way with more hard, sinewy work than book learning.

'When he was picked to tour England, he spent half an hour every night practising his autograph. Don't forget that, you collectors.'

On their arrival at Southampton, Gilchrist, along with the other fast bowlers Wes Hall, then only 19, and Tom Dewdney, the veteran of five Tests, generated a certain amount of press interest. 'He is the panther on the kill,' reported the *Daily Herald.*

'The tornado is no climatic term but a human one – one only five feet, seven inches high and turning the scales at only just over nine and a half stone, yet reckoned a major single menace to home victories on the tour ahead.

'The man is Roy Gilchrist, also known as "Black Panther", and the English batsmen are being warned in advance that anything can happen after he takes a deceptively slow walk to start his 23-yard [sic] run. Then, as one specialist describes it in terms almost calculated to stand a batsman's hair on end, he is off like a tornado, finishing with a four-yard leap into his delivery stride and a lightning cartwheel of his glistening mahogany arms. Sometimes, the ball roars away towards the first or even second slip, sometimes it seems aimed more at fine leg than the stumps. But four balls out of six are on target and a batsman hoping to ease himself in gently is likely to find his stumps uprooted before he has brought down his bat.'

He gave notice of his hostility in a warm-up game against E.W. Swanton's XI at Eastbourne when he twice hit Surrey batsman Micky Stewart; then, in his third game, against Essex at Ilford, one of his deliveries climbed far over opening batsman Dickie Dodds and wicketkeeper Alexander and sped off to the boundary, hitting the sightscreen first bounce. 'I hardly saw it before I heard the crash and saw the umpire signal four vertical wides,' recalled Sobers, who reckoned that he'd never seen bowling so fast and fierce. During the chill of the early season, Gilchrist was nursed very carefully, so that by the time of the first Test at the end of May, he'd played in only three of the eight first-class games and, with his accuracy awry, his analysis of one wicket for 155 runs off 55 overs was hardly inspiring. With such limited success it is perhaps surprising that he should have been picked for the Test, but with Hall and Dewdney struggling to adapt to local conditions, he was destined to lead the attack with only Worrell's military medium at the other end.

Batting first on an easy-paced wicket at Edgbaston, England spurned the opportunity to take the initiative. Gilchrist soon had opener Brian Close caught behind when he sparred at a short ball that deviated and he worked up a fair pace and bounce. Somewhat erratic in his opening overs, he later proved a steady foil to spinner

Sonny Ramadhin in an unbroken post-prandial spell of 17 overs in which he bowled wicketkeeper Godfrey Evans, fading only at the end when tailender Fred Trueman flogged him for several boundaries.

England's failure to read the wily Ramadhin, who took 7-49, proved their undoing as they slumped to 186 all out. Consigned to two days in the field, they appeared down and out as the West Indies, led by Collie Smith's 161, posted a first-innings lead of 288. In the final session of the day, Gilchrist, bowling very fast, struck Close a nasty blow on the finger and dismissed him early on the fourth morning to leave England 113/3. He also gave Peter May an uncomfortable time, particularly with deliveries just short of a length, but the England captain survived and, together with Colin Cowdrey, orchestrated a fightback. Learning from the lesson of the first innings, they resolved to get on to the front foot and play Ramadhin as an off-spinner. This would enable them to protect their stumps and allow Ramadhin's leg breaks to pass by harmlessly across their bats. With the umpires totally unresponsive to the numerous lbw appeals, Cowdrey in particular felt able to pad away any delivery Ramadhin pitched on and outside the off stump. His tactics, while highly controversial, proved extremely effective, since Ramadhin, bowled into the ground for a marathon 98 overs by his captain, began to lose his mastery and was never the same bowler again.

Gilchrist's absence on the final day because of a twisted ankle, sustained in a collision with the boundary board, only added to West Indies' woes. According to May, 'Gilchrist was fast enough and unpredictable enough to cause an element of surprise when he produced a good one and we were undoubtedly helped when he limped off the field during the day.' Increasingly in control, May and Cowdrey went remorselessly on, adding a record-breaking 411 for the fourth wicket, and when the former declared at 583/4, he'd taken his score to 285 not out.

Left 296 to win in two hours and 20 minutes, the demoralised tourists faced a gruelling examination from the England attack and were thankful to hang on for a draw at 72/7.

Injury kept Gilchrist out of the next three games and although he only managed one wicket against Sussex, there was no question of him missing the second Test. On the notorious Lord's ridge, which proved a great help to the quicker bowlers, West Indies erred badly by going into the match with one genuine paceman. Batting first, they were no match for Trevor Bailey's seamers and were all out for 127.

Their bowlers struck back immediately. Worrell trapped debutant Don Smith lbw and Gilchrist, in his most impressive spell of the tour, dismissed Tom Graveney and May, both without scoring, the latter to a ball that flew horribly close to his face, leaving England 34/3. As he and Worrell began to tire, opener Peter Richardson counter-attacked most effectively, before Gilchrist returned to bowl him for 76 just before the close.

When Bailey was out immediately the next morning, West Indies were back in the game. Gilchrist, working up great pace, rapped Close on the pads and thigh three balls in succession, inducing vociferous appeals from the large West Indian contingent in a capacity crowd, and had him groping outside the off stump. He also hit Cowdrey on the gloves several times with nasty lifters, but never once did Cowdrey flinch and helped by dire catching, he and Evans added 174 for the seventh wicket. Evans was missed an astounding eight times, twice off Gilchrist, who began to vent his frustration on him and Cowdrey with some vicious deliveries, two of which struck Cowdrey painful blows on the thigh. 'Godfrey, if you are going to lash at this bloke and keep getting tickles, for heaven's sake don't let's take a single,' Cowdrey admonished him. 'I keep getting these bouncers. They're very dangerous indeed.' While Cowdrey rated him the most venomous bowler he ever faced, Evans thought him 'fast, not over-intelligent, hostile and dangerous'. The surprised single or edged four left him 'pawing the ground in frustration'. And from the slips Worrell said, 'Godfrey, please stop slashing at Gilly. I'm frightened to death in the slips here.'

In retrospect Gilchrist came to appreciate that the Lord's wicket wasn't conducive to great speed and that he erred by trying to bowl too quick. 'The stuff I was pushing through was seaming *behind* the wicket, it was going so fast. But, in turn, Bailey used that little old green wicket like a master, heaving the ball down like it was dynamite. If I had had Bailey's cricketing sense, then those four wickets of mine might have been eight.'

Thanks to Cowdrey's 152, England made 424 to win by an innings and remained dominant for the rest of the series.

Gilchrist continued to show his potential against Derbyshire at Chesterfield. After the tourists had been dismissed for 115 in their first innings, he struck back by taking 5-41, troubling everyone, not least Derbyshire captain Donald Carr. 'Donald was an excellent player against fast bowling, very good on the back foot and at pulling the ball,' recalled team-mate Edwin Smith. 'But that day, when he made 21, Gilchrist bowled one which was far too quick for him.'

Gilchrist followed up with two further wickets in the second innings when Derbyshire, set 281 to win, capitulated for 117, providing a real fillip to the tourists before the third Test at Trent Bridge.

On a flat wicket that offered the bowlers nothing, England batted first and flourished against an eight-man attack. Graveney hit 258, dispatching Gilchrist with silky timing whenever he overpitched, and Richardson and May also scored centuries in their 619/6 declared. Despite Worrell's marathon 191 not out, the tourists were forced to follow on and at 89/5 they appeared doomed before a magnificent 168 from Collie Smith and a solid 61 from John Goddard kept their hopes alive. When they were finally all out for 367, England needed 121 to win in 17 overs and, after a hostile Gilchrist dismissed Richardson cheaply, they played out time.

By the end of the game there were private mutterings about Gilchrist's suspect action in an era when throwing was becoming a blight on the game. Calling him a 'brutal' bowler, Cowdrey struggled to distinguish between the perfectly fair delivery and his really fast bouncer and his yorker, delivered from wide of the crease, which he found terrifying. He wrote, 'Although a number of umpires studied this with great care, his arm never appeared to bend, and it remained something of a mystery. ... The occasional really fast ball breaks the law. How can any umpire be expected to cope with this?' It was indeed a real conundrum for umpires and while his action remained a matter of some debate thereafter, not least in the leagues, he was by no means the only suspect who survived the general purge of the throwers in the early 1960s.

Gilchrist enjoyed success against Somerset at Taunton. After most of the first day was lost to bad weather, the West Indians were bowled out for 78 in saturnine conditions on the second day, but he fought back with a hostile spell that evening when Gilchrist was close to unplayable. Somerset opener Bill Alley reckoned he was the fastest bowler he ever faced as the ball flew off the bat for a couple of fours. 'I can honestly say I knew next to nothing about them. I don't think I have ever been so frightened as a batsman.'

At the other end Wes Hall was just as intimidating. Having taken evasive action against a number of his bouncers, Alley confronted him and said, 'You know darn well you won't get me out this way.' 'I know, man,' Hall grinned, 'but it sure gives me a kick to see your face.'

With the county reeling at 27/4, the 20-year-old Ken Palmer was sent in as nightwatchman and survived to the close at 38/5.

The next morning, he faced a full onslaught from both Gilchrist and Hall, taking many a blow on the body, but he refused to buckle and when he was finally run out for 23 at 87/7, he left to appreciative applause from the members.

In the dressing room his gallantry was widely admired by his team-mates as the full extent of his bruising became visible, but as he went to remove his box, he suddenly realised that he'd forgotten to insert it in the first place.

Boosted by his second five-wicket haul of the tour, Gilchrist approached the Headingley Test in confident mood. At practice the day before, he met Jim Laker, who later accused him of bowling illegally, and greeted him in his cheerful way. 'You're a nice man,' he told him confidently. 'I keep the ball up to you. But that Trueman, with his horrible language, I bounce them at him,' a comment that alluded to an incident in the Lord's Test when the Yorkshireman had bowled short at him.

Admirably though Gilchrist bowled in the game, it counted for little in England's overwhelming victory. Once again, the West Indian batting failed dismally against the home attack, led by paceman Peter Loader, who crowned his performance of 6-36 with a hat-trick to finish off the innings, Gilchrist being the final victim. As he came in to bat a hush descended around the ground which was shattered by the wildest outburst of cheering when he missed a straight ball and had his stumps re-arranged.

All out for 142, West Indies fought back well on the second morning and when Gilchrist sent Graveney's middle stump flying yards back, forcing the wicketkeeper Alexander to take evasive action, England were teetering at 42/3. Although slightly wayward in length, he continued to cause May and Cowdrey some anxious moments before the former took control with some imperious driving. He, Cowdrey and David Sheppard all scored half-centuries to put England firmly in control. 'We were all glad to see the Rev. Sheppard do well, which might sound crazy,' wrote Gilchrist rather out of character, 'but there is not a finer man in cricket than him. None of the swearing, none of the back-chat; and no grumbling if any of that goes on around him either.'

During the latter stages of the England innings, Gilchrist caused a stir with the Yorkshire crowd by removing Trueman's cap with the fastest bouncer that Laker had ever seen, revenge for the bouncer that Trueman had given him at Lord's. It shot past a couple of inches from his nose even before he had properly lifted from his stance. 'Trueman went white and – believe it or not – said nothing,' Gilchrist recalled. 'It takes something, believe me, to render Trueman speechless.'

'They don't seem to have heard of the fast bowlers' union in the West Indies,' Trueman later wrote, referring to a previous incident when he'd been bounced by Barbadian paceman Frank King and forgetting his own flouting of that convention to Gilchrist, but he never had the chance to get his revenge.

Despite Gilchrist's efforts and 7-70 from Worrell, England posted a lead of 137 before dismissing the tourists for 132 to win by an innings.

Influenza forced Gilchrist to miss the final Test in which, once again, the West Indies batting sank without trace on an atrocious wicket at The Oval. Their defeat by an innings and 237 runs capped a disastrous tour in which little had gone right. Although his team had been outplayed in all departments, Goddard did take heart from Gilchrist's showing and, although guilty of over-bowling him in long spells, he predicted an auspicious future for him. *Wisden*, too, was complimentary, commenting that 'Gilchrist was menacing by virtue of his genuine pace and ability to produce a bouncer as venomous as any sent down by the opposition', but, according to Trevor Bailey, he found Gilchrist easy to play provided one got into line. He did little with the ball in the air or off the pitch. *The Sunday Gleaner*'s Harvey Day opined that the West Indies selectors had asked too much of Gilchrist because of his sheer speed – especially given their error of bringing over three fast bowlers with practically no experience of first-class cricket. He was a real discovery and might one day, if he could find a partner equally as good, run through the finest sides. 'He is very fast. But he lacks guile and doesn't know how to conceal his slower ball like Loader does. His bumper, which flies from the middle of the pitch over the batsman, holds a danger only for the wicketkeeper.'

Gilchrist himself admitted to learning a lot by bowling to the likes of May, Cowdrey and Graveney, whom he particularly rated, in English conditions, appreciating that mere strength and stamina weren't enough. After the tourists' match against Yorkshire, he met Bill Bowes, the former England fast bowler, who told him he could be a fine prospect if he cut down his 26-yard run and bowled a slightly fuller length. He suggested 18 yards and Gilchrist operated thereafter between 18 and 22 yards, while occasionally reverting to his longer run to intimidate batsmen.

Although Gilchrist had acquitted himself respectably on the field, the same could hardly be said of his conduct off it, not least his gaucheness at official receptions or his inclination to speak out of turn. In the opinion of Walcott, the vice-captain, he was difficult for any captain to handle. 'He had the ability to be as quick as everyone and he was given every chance. He was uneducated and gave the impression that he felt everyone was against him,' a point underlined in British Guiana the previous year when one of his team-mates mocked his attempt to sign his autograph, a slur which raised his hackles. In his biography of Wes Hall, the author Paul Akeroyd relates an incident before the tourists' first county match against Worcestershire which Hall felt enhanced Gilchrist's insecurity. On an evening stroll through Worcester, two police officers who'd welcomed the party and noted Gilchrist's lingering detachment from his team-mates were asked by Denis Atkinson to participate in a prank. Having suggested to Gilchrist that he catch up with the rest of the party, the officers then asked Atkinson if he knew Gilchrist. Atkinson said that he had never seen him in his life. 'At that point, Wes saw that Gilchrist was overcome with panic,' wrote Akeroyd.

'Gilly was frozen, in a state of shock … until the guys started laughing and hugging him; letting him know that they were only fooling around. They would never have known how deeply their little joke would affect Gilly … Genuine light-hearted ribbing and malicious aggravation stirred the same reaction, because young Roy never learned how to differentiate between the two.'

Given his lack of confidence and literary skills – certain team-mates had to help him read and write letters – any trip to England would pose challenges to a young man from his background, and he wasn't well served by the tour leadership. The idea of joint managers didn't work; the players thought that Worrell should have been captain and with the party dividing into cliques a unity of purpose was missing. According to Worrell, there was little tact dealing with the younger players and it was depressing to see them struggle in unfamiliar conditions without proper help and advice, a view which Gilchrist endorsed. He complained that no one told him how to seam the ball properly or how to get accustomed to English wickets. 'I had to get used to the facts of life the hard and long way, and in the meantime a lot of batsmen got a lot of runs too easily.'

Gilchrist's troubled relationship with some of his superiors surfaced at various stages of the tour. Edwin Smith, the Derbyshire off-spinner, recalled Gilchrist bowling bouncers to Cliff Gladwin at Chesterfield and Walcott, who wasn't captaining the team, saying to him, 'Gilchrist, if you can't get 9, 10, 11 out without bowling a bouncer, put your sweater on.' His rift with Walcott came to a head late on in the tour at Canterbury. According to C.L.R. James, who was present, Gilchrist resented the failure of the stand-in captain to give him the new ball in the second innings and he didn't care who knew. During that same match, he became embroiled in a heated altercation with Weekes, who on learning that Gilchrist had accepted an offer to play league cricket in England the following summer, taunted him, as he'd done intermittently throughout the tour. Objecting to what was said to him, Gilchrist fought back and when Goddard overheard them in full flow, he asked them to explain themselves to the tour management that evening. As far as the two managers were concerned, Tom Peirce thought the spat more serious than Cecil de Caires, but after receiving apologies from both men, the incident was declared closed. Later, when the WICBC withheld half of Gilchrist's £150 tour bonus, Cecil Marley, a Jamaican representative on the board, insisted that his punishment had nothing to do with the incident with Weekes, but the board's failure to explain themselves fully drew criticism from Strebor Roberts. He wrote, 'But even on the face of his statement although admitting that Roy Gilchrist was penalised £75, Mr Marley has not said what was the nature of the offence Gilchrist committed which caused such drastic action to be taken against him; for it must have been something serious that made the board slice his bonus in two.'

Despite Roberts's call for a full statement from the board explaining the penalising of Gilchrist, nothing emerged until nearly two years later, following the decision to send him home from India for insubordination. Defending the board's ban on Gilchrist for the 1959/60 series against England, Marley claimed that in England in 1957, he was 'guilty of many acts of misconduct and one occasion went so far as to attack a member of his side'. Although there is no confirmation about the identity of the victim, this appears to have been the occasion when he allegedly attacked wicketkeeper Gerry Alexander with a knife. Many years later, when quizzed about the veracity of the allegations by his Thornham team-mates in the bar when tongues were loosened by a few beers, Gilchrist grinned and said it was a fork.

'If Gilchrist had played for WI before the last war, wrote *The Gleaner*'s Jack Anderson, 'what he was reported to have done in

England would have caused him to be shunned by even a Senior Cup cricket club, much less to play for Jamaica again.'

Interestingly enough, Gilchrist bore no bitterness towards Goddard. Although he acknowledged his tactical limitations as a captain, especially his over-reliance on Ramadhin, whom he thought overrated, he liked him and sympathised with his plight. He wrote, 'I felt sorry for John Goddard. Nothing he did would go right. He might have failed in his field-placing for Ramadhin as a lot of people have said, but when Cowdrey, May and Graveney caught up with our bowler there was no field-placing that could have saved him. And so Goddard got to feeling low. Who could blame him? Most of us felt like crying for him, for he always treated the youngest of us as if we were men, real men, and not just little bits of nothing to be shoved about. It is a pity some of the other players did not take notice of him. They would have learned a lot from him.

'When things go badly for the top men … there is a feeling of "we-can't-win-man" that sweeps through a side. And that defeatist feeling was pushed even higher by the fact that catches which players would have gobbled up at other times were put on the deck as though that was the way cricket should be played.'

It was to overcome that sense of defeatism that the West Indies selectors felt bound to take drastic action, with profound consequences for both Gilchrist and the team.

Chapter 3

Pummelling Pakistan

FOLLOWING THE debacle of the England tour and the retirement of Goddard, the WICBC offered the captaincy for the home series against Pakistan in early 1958 to Frank Worrell. When Worrell, a mature student at Manchester University, declined, putting his studies first (he also declined the leadership to India and Pakistan later that year), the board, ignoring the claims of their most senior players, Everton Weekes and Clyde Walcott, now turned to Gerry Alexander, a choice which won little support outside Jamaica.

The decision to overlook Weekes and Walcott for the captaincy stemmed partly from the recent tour of England, when both players had lost half of their bonuses, largely on the report of co-manager Cecil de Caires. As far as he was concerned, neither Weekes nor Walcott made any serious effort to get fit, bat themselves into form in the nets or provide any serious help to the younger players. Although his allegations were rightly refuted by his co-manager Tom Peirce, Weekes's first Barbadian captain, and later publicly disowned by the board following the threat of legal action, the damage had been done. By then both men had retired from international cricket – although Walcott did make a brief return against England two years later – leaving the field clear for Alexander.

A light-skinned Jamaican of European descent, and from a well-to-do family, Alexander was educated at Wolmer's Boys' School, Kingston, one of the leading schools in the Caribbean, and at Cambridge University, where he read veterinary medicine. A talented sportsman, he not only gained Blues in cricket and football, but also won an FA Amateur Cup medal for Pegasus, the team composed of Oxbridge students, in front of 100,000 at Wembley in 1953. He was a good enough full-back to play one game for the England amateur side against Bulgaria in 1956.

At a time when Jamaica was becoming a more open, socially mobile society and on the cusp of gaining independence, Alexander's appointment proved highly controversial, not least with Stollmeyer. It wasn't simply that, once again, the board had defied the march of history by appointing a privileged light-skinned man to captain the national side; Alexander also appeared to lack the necessary talent to succeed at Test level. He certainly had underperformed in the two Tests he'd played in England, failing to pick Ramadhin when keeping to him and scoring 11 runs in three completed innings, but once in charge he fully vindicated the board's faith. Not only did his batting and wicketkeeping improve beyond all recognition, he also proved a highly respected captain, not least for the way he fashioned a talented new side out of the ruins of the old.

A man of honour and dignity who espoused the ethical code of sportsmanship of the English public schools, he seemed the person to restore discipline to the ranks. Jackie Hendriks recalled that Alexander, several years his senior at Wolmer's, was his house captain when he, Hendriks, was captain of the under-12s. Having dismissed the opposition for 35 in one house match, the team then batted for a long time, aiming to earn house points with a big score. Finishing with 95, Hendriks felt very proud of himself for getting those points, only to be reprimanded by Alexander the following day. He told him that batting on indefinitely after dismissing the opposition cheaply wasn't cricket and that he was taking the house points away from him, a bitter lesson for Hendriks regarding the ethics of the game and respecting the opposition.

Fully aware of Worrell's claims to the captaincy, Alexander offered to make way for him for the 1959/60 home series against England, and when his leadership was subjected to a withering assault by the Marxist intellectual C.LR. James, he conducted himself with great dignity. He tactfully ceded the captaincy to Worrell for the forthcoming tour of Australia and, having assented to go as vice-captain, he proved the most loyal of deputies, valued for his tactical advice and his mentoring of the younger players. He also won accolades from opposing captain Richie Benaud for his outstanding wicketkeeping and batting in a series in which he headed the West Indies Test batting averages with 484 runs at 60.50, and from all-rounder Alan Davidson for his impeccable sportsmanship. On his retirement at the end of that tour, he pursued an eminent career as a veterinary surgeon for the Agriculture Ministry, becoming in time chief veterinary officer for the Jamaican government. He was president of Kingston Cricket Club, a Jamaican selector and a popular manager of the victorious West Indies 1974/75 tour to India, winning the appreciation of the captain Clive Lloyd for his help and encouragement in fostering an excellent team spirit. In 1982 Alexander was awarded Jamaica's Order of Distinction for his outstanding contribution to sport throughout the Caribbean and his death in 2011 left many bereft. Gary Sobers described him as a 'truly wonderful man whose heart and soul were in West Indies cricket' and his Jamaican team-mate Easton McMorris called him a gentleman of the old school.

Up against a talented Pakistan side, especially its formidable batting led by Hanif Mohammad, West Indies, with centuries from debutant Conrad Hunte and veteran Everton Weekes, ran up a formidable 579/9 declared in the first Test at Bridgetown, before unleashing Gilchrist in the closing minutes of the second day. Before the match, he'd been taunted in the nets with shouts of 'Go home' by local Barbadians, who accused him of going through the motions. Neither did his slight frame endear him to them, but this all changed with his opening spell. Running in at high speed, his first ball was a bouncer of such velocity that it was still climbing as it cleared wicketkeeper Alexander before crashing into a wall below the Challenor Stand on the full. 'I was watching from the stands as a 17-year-old schoolboy and my recollection is still vivid,' wrote the renowned West Indian cricket writer and broadcaster Tony Cozier. By now the crowd, beside themselves with excitement, roared even louder when Alexander and the slips turned and took three deliberate paces back before the next ball. 'You could hear a pin drop in Kensington,' Gilchrist later recalled with a smile, 'and I had a taxi full of presents waiting after the game.'

The next day, his lethal pace unnerved Pakistan to the extent that they were all out for 106 in 42.2 overs. Following on 473 behind, the openers, the diminutive Hanif and the hard-hitting Imtiaz Ahmed, found themselves back in the firing line. Galvanised by the crowd's vociferous support, Gilchrist continued to bowl very fast and had both openers dropped early on, Hanif from a rising ball that flew to slip. He then aimed one directly at Hanif's head, which Hanif countered by swaying out the way at the last moment. After one unavailing attempt to hook him, Walcott approached Hanif at the end of the over and said, 'Don't try to hook Gilchrist because he is too fast for you.' Imtiaz, however, wasn't to be deterred as he repeatedly pulled Gilchrist, who was battling severe eye pain from the glare of the sun, so much so that the doctor told him he would have to wear glasses. One of his bouncers glanced Imtiaz's chin, sending a chill down the spine of his team-mates who thought he'd been badly hurt, but Imtiaz stood his ground and hooked the next bouncer over the ropes. His fortitude won the admiration of Alexander, who later wrote that Imtiaz was the best Pakistan batsman he ever saw. 'At the start of the second innings, Gilchrist's first ball, a searing bouncer, kissed Imtiaz's chin before thudding into my gloves while he was still completing his shot. The slip cordon including Sobers all muttered this poor man is dead. The next blistering bouncer was flourished to the fence and from then Gilchrist went bouncer mad and Imtiaz hooked and pulled him with tremendous skill and authority till he had totally destroyed him.

'I have never seen a more devastating, destroying exhibition of hooking and pulling against such terrific pace. In fact, it was his total demoralisation of our main strike bowler making him absolutely ineffective, which paved the way for Hanif's 337 in that match.'

On a rapidly improving pitch, Imtiaz and Hanif gave their side the perfect start with an opening stand of 152, the latter finishing the day undefeated on 61. In blistering heat, and in some pain given the blows he sustained from Gilchrist on his unprotected thigh, Hanif batted throughout the whole of the fourth and fifth days, by which time he advanced to 270 out of Pakistan's 525/3. When he was eventually dismissed for 337, his remarkable 970-minute epic, the longest innings ever played in first-class cricket, ensured his side a draw. But there was a price to be paid for his heroics, since those 16 hours at the crease exposed him to 40 overs of Gilchrist. Michael Manley in his *A History of West Indies Cricket* wrote, 'For hour after hour, Hanif dealt with balls in excess of 90 miles per hour, rearing past a head fractionally withdrawn at the last moment. Who can tell what tiny increments of fear were lodged in the back of his mind, as lodge they must in the back of the mind of every batsman who has to face really hostile bowling.'

Pakistan's fightback forced all those critics such as J.S. Barker, the cricket correspondent of the *Trinidad Guardian*, who'd written them off at the end of the second day, to eat their words. He took his ire out on Gilchrist, despite his unstinting efforts on a docile surface, writing that his failure to stay the course was at least as important a factor in West Indies' failure to press home their advantage as any other.

'Gilchrist's pace, as I have said before, could be Alexander's match- and series-winning asset. But, if this slightly-built bowler … is to produce his best on our unforgiving wickets over a period of six days, then he has to go into training like a race-horse, not as an ass … Gilchrist could not raise a gallop on the final day.'

Barker's allegation that Gilchrist wasn't fit, in addition to causing deep resentment in Trinidad, was strongly refuted by Strebor Roberts. He wrote, 'It is untrue to say that the West Indian team was not fit, and particularly Gilchrist, who had to go from fine leg to fine leg and yet on that last day I saw him chasing balls to the boundary, and so were other members of the West Indies side who stuck to their task nobly after hunting leather for four days.'

Following Hanif's 337, Gilchrist said to his team-mates, 'Watch me against him next time,' and he proved as good as his word as he peppered him with bouncers during Pakistan's first innings in the second Test at Port-of-Spain. Hanif made only 30 but some stubborn resistance from their lower order prompted Gilchrist to bowl a bouncer at their number 11, Mahmood Hussain, which elicited boos from the home crowd and prompted further criticism from Barker. He later apologised to the batsman at the request of Alexander. (Mahmood Hussain told Gilchrist he, too, could bowl fast.)

West Indies built upon a lead of 43 and set their opponents 356 for victory. A second-wicket stand of 130 between Hanif and Saeed Ahmed gave them an outside chance and they started the final day on 161/3 with Hanif still at the crease. On a dank morning conducive to swing bowling, Gilchrist immediately struck the first blow by bowling Wazir Mohammad, Hanif's elder brother, for 0 before unnerving Hanif with a liberal supply of bouncers. Many years later Hanif admitted that facing him was at times terrifying.

'Gilchrist's fearsome and threatening pace had totally shattered my confidence. Thank God I had stopped hooking him. I will always remember a delivery from him. It pitched short and kept on coming at me. I swayed, tilting my small frame back, but was caught on the wrong foot, and didn't know which side to move. It whizzed past, barely missing me. I do not know how I survived it. If it had hit me on the face or head, I would surely have died. That delivery still returns to haunt me in my nightmares.'

'I've never known to this day how he managed to get out of the way of the angry red leather,' noted Rohan Kanhai, who was fielding at silly mid-on. 'He turned two shades lighter and literally stood dithering in the crease.'

After a stay of 273 minutes, Hanif, on 81, aimed to cut Gilchrist and was supremely caught by a diving Sobers in the gully. Gilchrist then clean bowled Fazal Mahmood next ball and his spell of 3-16 from seven overs, an exhibition of sustained accuracy, transformed the game in West Indies' favour. With off-spinner Lance Gibbs mopping up the tail, they won by 120 runs.

The third Test at Kingston will always be remembered for Sobers's record-breaking 365 not out as West Indies, in reply to Pakistan's first innings of 328, decimated their depleted attack to score 790/3 declared. On a very fast wicket and cheered on by his home crowd, Gilchrist's raw pace accounted for Hanif cheaply in both innings, a significant factor in his side's comprehensive innings victory, but he didn't have things entirely his own way, since he only took three wickets in the match. In the first innings, Imtiaz attacked him with gusto during his 122 and, in the second innings, the resistance was led by Wazir Mohammad, who hit Gilchrist for four boundaries in one over in his defiant 106. Frightened by Gilchrist and his habit of staring at a batsman and bowling even faster if a Pakistani deigned to hit him for four, Wazir told his team-mates not to look at him in these circumstances, a tactic which slightly improved matters.

In the fourth Test at Georgetown, Gilchrist repeated his feat of the previous Test by dismissing Hanif in both innings, despite the latter's move down the order to afford him some protection from the new ball. On a plumb wicket, Pakistan batted first and made 408 with Hanif scoring 79, but he never looked happy facing Gilchrist. Having taken many a blow on the body, he was bowled by him retreating to square leg in what many spectators regarded as the most hostile spell of fast bowling ever seen at the Bourda Oval. When Gilchrist followed up by bowling Wallis Mathias the bails ended up six yards from the boundary.

His performance won the approval of the British Guyanese journalist Pryor Jonas who wrote of his devilish aggression, not least his hostile glare at the umpire for rejecting his demand for lbw. 'Yes, Roy Gilchrist … the entire Windies attack is built on your wiry frame. I never cease to wonder at the momentum and venom you so successfully work up. It may be true that you tend to be erratic; it may be true, also, that in your moment of wrath you overdo the bouncer (and the beamer). But surely these are remedial faults in your urgent quest for mastery over that upstart of a batsman. So I salute you, Roy Gilchrist.'

Having conceded a first-innings lead of two, Pakistan began their second innings in tentative mood. Once Hanif appeared at 44/2, Gilchrist was recalled to the attack and having ruffled him again with his extreme pace, he had him spectacularly caught at cover by Ivan Madray for 14. With Wazir making 97 not out and A.H. Kardar 56, the tourists batted resolutely to set West Indies 317 for victory, only then to suffer a serious setback to their leading bowler Fazal Mahmood. On the evidence of this series, Fazal thought Gilchrist the fastest bowler he'd seen. He wrote, 'Gilly had a very unique habit. For the first ball, he would appear from behind the screen, and run up to the bowling crease amid chants of "Gilly, Gilly."' When sent in by Kardar to bat at number eight in the first innings, Fazal recalled Gilchrist fielding at third man. He walked up to him and asked, 'Have you been sent in or have you come in on your own?' 'Sent,' was his reply. 'Okay,' he declared, and after that he didn't bounce him.

Fazal did, however, receive such an excruciating blow on the knee from Gilchrist in the second innings of the fourth Test that it required several injections in hospital to relieve the pain and limited him to just four overs in West Indies' second innings. The absence of Pakistan's leading bowler proved crucial. Led by centuries from Hunte and Sobers, his second of the game, the home side strolled to an eight-wicket victory to give them an unassailable 3-0 lead in the series.

An ankle injury limited Gilchrist to seven overs in the final Test at Port-of-Spain, where Pakistan gained a consolation innings victory, but this apparently wasn't the whole story. In his autobiography, he stated that the real reason for his absence was his desire to give fellow paceman Jaswick Taylor the opportunity to stake his claim for a place on West Indies' forthcoming tour to India and Pakistan and, to general delight, Taylor's five wickets gained him selection.

Reviewing the series in the round, Kardar blamed the failure of his batsmen to come to terms with the West Indian pace attack, especially Gilchrist, whose 21 wickets exceeded any other bowler on either side and came at an average of 30.28. He had improved throughout by bowling more at the stumps, while reserving his faster ball as a surprise weapon. Kardar admitted that Gilchrist had upset Hanif in the second Test at Port-of-Spain by getting more out of the wicket than he had in Barbados. 'Hanif seemed to be running away from the lifting ball. This tendency was more noticeable in the Jamaica Test – so much so that by the time we played the fourth Test Hanif had got into a psychological tangle and was in no mood despite the placid nature of the wicket to come to arms with Gilchrist.'

The Gleaner's Jack Anderson wrote, 'The reward of Gilchrist's England tour was seen early, but by the third Test it seemed to have been affecting his ego, and he was forgetting that there were fielders on the field and only Gilchrist was to bowl as fast as possible! We hope this is temporary.'

There were other concerns about his attitude. According to the WICBC, he had been guilty of grave misconduct at the Queen's Park Hotel, Port-of-Spain, and was 'very nearly sent home'. It needed a profound apology by the president and secretary of the WICBC in a personal meeting with the hotel management and a promise by Gilchrist to mend his ways to settle the matter. Nevertheless, before the tour to India and Pakistan that autumn, manager Berkeley Gaskin reminded him that, as far as the WICBC were concerned, he was on his final warning and that he would face the consequences should he transgress again. 'I knew then that my respect for those in charge had gone', Gilchrist later recalled, 'and that the board did not think much of me.' The seeds of later trouble had been well and truly sown.

Chapter 4

Beamed into Exile

WEST INDIES' win over Pakistan enhanced Alexander's authority as a captain and wicketkeeper of some stature, and with Worrell once again unavailable for the tour to India and Pakistan because of his studies, it was entirely understandable that he should continue in charge. The series in the Caribbean also saw the emergence of Gilchrist, Sobers and Hunte as players of true international class. The team's rebuilding continued on their subsequent tour when, following the retirement of Weekes and Walcott, both overlooked for the captaincy, the likes of Wes Hall, Rohan Kanhai, Basil Butcher, Collie Smith and Joe Solomon came of age. Nothing better illustrated their supremacy in India than their formidable opening attack of Gilchrist and Hall, who proved a constant threat even on lifeless pitches. Raised in these conditions, the Indian batsmen weren't used to facing such lightning pace and, consequently, they played it with little confidence or skill. At nets on arrival at the beginning of the tour, it was Gilchrist who commanded all the attention, especially when bowling a series of bouncers, a couple of which flew over the net. He was nearly twice as fast as any other bowler. When Ramakant Desai, a scrawny 19-year-old, was introduced to Gilchrist as India's fastest bowler, the latter thought it some kind of a joke.

After a gentle opener against the Services XI at Poona, Gilchrist and Hall hit their straps in the second match against the Ranji Trophy champions Baroda, taking 12 wickets between them. Such was their hostility that the former India captain Vijay Hazare, who bagged a pair, watched his young batsmen fear for their lives. Even former Test batsman Deepak Shodan, who relished playing fast bowling, recalled the battering he took from Gilchrist and Hall in that game during his innings of 23 and 25. By the end of it, the home side looked like visitors to the outpatients' department of a hospital. 'Not since 1932/33 has a cricket field seen such intimidation,' wrote the distinguished British-Indian sports writer Mihir Bose. 'Cricket, a delicate game, was converted into warfare where one side, the Indians, only had pea shooters, and the other side the latest machine-guns. It was surprising that in this era, long before the wearing of helmets or other protective gear had been adopted, nobody was killed.'

Yet for all his pace and venom, Gilchrist, with his English experience behind him, was learning to vary his pace according to the conditions and become more accurate. Bowling within himself on occasions, he took a number of cheap wickets in the early provincial matches, although two broken stumps when bowling Maharashtra's Ramachandra Salvi and Vasant Ranjane gave notice of what awaited the Indian batsmen. He also had the added luxury of real pace at the other end now that his room-mate Hall had developed into a formidable opening bowler.

Of towering frame, the muscular Hall, with his long, athletic run-up, bulging eyes, gold crucifix glistening on his chest and classical action presented an awesome sight to opposition batsmen. Three years younger than Gilchrist, he'd struggled in England in 1957, although the pair did establish a close rapport. The two first met in the Test trial earlier that year when Hall hit Gilchrist for consecutive fours and a towering six which brought a threat of retaliation from an aggrieved bowler. Yet by rooming together in England they became firm friends, the amiable Hall understanding Gilchrist's background and appreciating the technical advice he received from the man he considered his mentor. He wrote, 'You could not help but feel bright with Gilly around. He would come out with hundreds of sayings which would make even Frankenstein laugh, and he was always ready with a sound word of advice if you needed it.'

That advice continued in India when Hall in his debut series fulfilled his great potential. He later recalled, 'My fondest memory of Gilchrist was that in 1958 in India, when I was a late replacement in the side.

'I was obviously behind many other fast bowlers like Gilchrist, Eric Atkinson and Jaswick Taylor. From the first day I bowled in the nets, however, Gilly impressed upon me that he was sure I would make the team.'

On the evening before the Baroda match, Gilchrist asked Hall who was the fastest bowler in the world.

'You are, Gilly.'

'Oh, I like you, College Boy!' (A term he used to describe anyone who had been to senior school.) 'By the end of this tour, I will make *you* number two!'

Gilchrist then proceeded to tell Hall he wanted him to bowl around the wicket, a ploy that found little favour with the latter, who'd never bowled around the wicket before and was reluctant to experiment at a time when his Test place was far from secure. He protested but Gilchrist was insistent, explaining that batsmen facing Hall would shuffle across the crease towards the off side to get into line with his outswingers or to avoid short-pitched deliveries, thereby presenting himself – bowling fast inswingers from the other end – with lbw opportunities.

Hall reluctantly consented to the plan and noting its effectiveness in the Baroda game, he continued to employ it throughout the tour.

The best of friends, they helped each other with tactical advice and plotted the downfall of many an opponent in a series in which, together, they captured 56 wickets. Gilchrist wrote, 'An idea of just how fast we really were, came home to me when Alexander put me in the leg-slip arc when Wes was bowling. One got through, but, as I was starting to cup my hands to stop it, it had gone straight past me, cracked the boundary fence and rebounded back to me. All I had to do was bend down and pick it up! That was enough for me. I walked straight into the covers and told the fellow there that we were switching places – I was there to bowl them out, not get knocked out by old Wes. I did not ask Alexander if I could go, but, man, I sure was going!'

While West Indies approached the first Test in confident mood, the home side, who'd never beaten their opponents in ten previous Tests, were blighted by regional rivalries among their selectors. Owing to the influence of the chairman of selectors Lala Amarnath, Ghulam Ahmed, a fine off-spinner but past his prime, was appointed captain, only then to withdraw days before the first Test because of a knee injury. He was replaced by veteran batsman Polly Umrigar, by no means everyone's choice, the first of four Indian captains during the series.

On a placid Bombay surface, West Indies batted first and made 227 before Hall and Gilchrist took centre stage. Racing in to bowl from near the boundary to the accompanying roar of the crowd, they posed a persistent danger to batsmen poorly equipped to face such pace, not least their tendency to duck under bouncers or move away and expose leg stump. Only Umrigar with 55 suggested permanence before he was out to the best ball of the day, his middle stump uprooted by Gilchrist. 'He [Gilchrist] was the fastest bowler I played against, a real terror,' recollected debutant Chandu Borde, India's find of the series and, according to Gilchrist, easily their best batsman. 'We had never played that kind of bowling before. His motto was to hit the batsman so that he would be scared and get out.

'Hall was fast in patches and used to mix his pace cleverly. Gilchrist was fast all the time and had tremendous stamina … In the Bombay Test he bowled virtually throughout the final day. Gilchrist's bouncer was very dangerous. It used to skid on to you and the aim was unerring. He often bowled four bouncers in an over.

'Gilchrist was a different sort of character. We were sitting and chit-chatting one day and he said: "My first objective is to hit the batsman. The moment I hit him I know I've got them. Then they'll run away from my bowling and it's an easy thing for me."'

'In India in 1958/9, Wes and Gilchrist were feared by the Indians,' wrote Sobers. 'They bowled so fast. The first time he kept to Gilly, wicketkeeper Gerry Alexander couldn't believe he was so quick. One or two Indians were "absent ill" on the scorecard in that series.'

According to Kanhai, Gilchrist was exceptionally powerful for such a small man. He could pound away for over after over in the blistering heat without ever showing any signs of tiredness. 'This great strength has amazed the critics over the years and baffled India's top doctors. I remember one distinguished heart specialist eyeing Gilchrist closely during a reception. He admitted he'd love to examine him. "That man intrigues me," he said with a wistful look. "I'd give anything to see the size of his heart. It must be big, really big."'

Dismissing India for 152, Gilchrist taking 4-39, the West Indies gained a lead of 75 on first innings and were able to declare, setting their opponents 399 to win in nine and a half hours. They made occupation of the crease their sole objective and although opener Pankaj Roy floundered against Gilchrist, he survived, due to woeful slip catching, to make 90 in over seven hours. (He later felt the need to leave surreptitious gifts for Gilchrist at the team hotel.) 'But I think poor Pankaj must still be having nightmares about that innings,' Gilchrist wrote. 'He just never knew where the ball was coming to him; he did not know which side to run to, to escape our bowling. Snick after snick went into the slips, but they just would not stick … And Roy went on ducking and dodging a bombardment that would have opened up Cassino! The way he did his "dance" sure did not make the other Indian batsmen keen to race out to face us. But they hung on, man, although it was not the prettiest sight I have ever seen.

'Those Indians were really on the "hop". I sprinkled a lot of bouncers in my bowling, and a beamer or two for good luck; … Real little Indian rubber men, those batsmen, the way they bounced about. You could almost hear the sigh of relief from Hardikar and Ramchand, the not-out batsmen, when the umpire called time.' Gilchrist was all set to play in the next match against

Central Districts at Jabalpur when he informed Gaskin that he was suffering from gonorrhoea contracted from a prostitute in Bombay. The news bred panic at the team hotel as players fretted about the possible contamination of towels and, that evening, they were warned about the high incidence of VD in India and the danger it posed. Consequently, anyone found visiting brothels or consorting with prostitutes would face severe disciplinary sanctions. Gilchrist was treated successfully in Jabalpur but, several weeks later, two days before the third Test at Calcutta, he reported a recurrence of the infection. Again, he was treated and passed fit but, unknown to the management at the time, he once again required a doctor in Delhi having apparently entertained a prostitute in his room during the fifth Test.

Gilchrist didn't play in the second Test supposedly because of a pulled muscle which concealed the real reason for his omission – his lack of self-control and irreverent attitude towards his captain – a disciplinarian of the old school whose curt, authoritarian form of leadership lacked Worrell's sensitivity towards troubled individuals.

What coloured Gilchrist's view of his captain was Alexander's treatment of Ivan Madray, a promising young leg-spinner of Indo-Guyanese stock from the remote sugar plantation of Port Mourant, the birthplace of several prominent cricketers. Making his Test debut against Pakistan in the second Test at Port-of-Spain earlier that year, Madray's frustration at Alexander's failure to take a couple of chances off his bowling led to an unusual request. 'Skipper,' he said, 'Rohan [Kanhai] understands my bowling. Let Rohan keep.'

Understandably slighted by such brazen temerity from a debutant, Alexander reacted out of character by not only under-bowling Madray in his two Tests, but also by barely speaking to him.

Shunned by his captain and team-mates and feeling increasingly depressed, Madray found a staunch ally in Gilchrist. The two of them had become friends during the Jamaica–British Guiana game in 1956 and during the Port-of-Spain Test against Pakistan, Gilchrist took him off to a bar to try to raise his spirits. His kindness was much appreciated but was to little avail because, missing out to leg-spinner Willy Rodriguez on the subsequent tour to India and Pakistan, Madray emigrated to Britain to take up a coaching appointment.

It should be noted that, on the field, Alexander's steely desire to win, seen by some Indian journalists as too tolerant of his side's short-pitched bowling, his immaculate wicketkeeping and his personal courage commanded Gilchrist's respect. He wrote, 'By the time Alexander arrived in India he was looking real good; just the man to take our sort of bowling and not the tricky spin of Ramadhin and Valentine alone. And whatever else I have said about Alexander he certainly had guts; lots and lots of guts.

'He almost did away with first slip. He just went flying in that direction and did the other boy's job for him. Bang, bang, bang went Alexander on to the ground on that right arm until it was raw. And he went off the field to get his arm doctored and bandaged up so that he could come running back to do his daredevil act all over again.'

Alexander in turn admired Gilchrist's pace and relentless stamina on those flat, sluggish pitches. One night at Bombay, after bowling all day, the West Indians went to a dance staged in their honour and Gilchrist engaged in some energetic rock and roll. 'How do you do it, Gilly?' Alexander asked him. 'I'm on my knees, man,' to which Gilchrist replied, 'I'm fit, skip.'

Cricketing respect aside, there was little the two men had in common. While the self-effacing Alexander squirmed at Gilchrist's brazen self-confidence as he derisively dissected the frailties of the Indian batting, Gilchrist increasingly felt that Alexander looked down on him. He wrote, 'The trouble with the whole outlook between us was that I always had a feeling that Gilly from the plantation could never be on the same level as Gerry from the varsity. While fellows knew me as Roy Gilchrist, or Gilly, everyone seemed to regard Gerry as Mr F.C.M. Alexander, Cambridge University and West Indies.

'I felt that maybe it was Mr F.C.M. Alexander who should be making me feel at home, rather than the other way round. He had his pals, and I just was not one of them. And maybe you have gathered that I don't go chasing people to shake their hand if I feel the other fellow is not all that interested.'

Yet while Gilchrist emphasised the class divide to explain his rift with Alexander – ironic that it wasn't an issue with the more patrician Goddard in England – we shouldn't exaggerate this. There were plenty of his team-mates who came from similar backgrounds: Kanhai, Butcher and Solomon were brought up on the same sugar plantation in British Guiana; Ramadhin was an orphan from a sugar plantation in Trinidad; Hunte was born in a one-room house in Barbados, the eldest of nine children; Sobers was the son of a merchant seaman; Hall was the son of a boxer and Collie Smith was raised in Kingston's slums, and while they might have kept their distance from Alexander off the field – captains in those days tended to be remote figures – it didn't diminish their mutual respect.

Indeed, one of Alexander's cardinal virtues as captain was to forge a new sense of camaraderie in the team after the divisions in England in 1957.

Gilchrist's clash with Alexander stemmed from his general dislike of authority, evident in the Kingston Test against Pakistan when his failure to obey his captain's instructions prompted his home crowd to shout to Alexander to 'take him off!' The latter also disapproved of his hard-nosed ethos which flouted the spirit of the game and upset opponents.

During a discussion in a train compartment early on the tour to India, Gilchrist shocked his manager with his admission that he wouldn't mind killing a batsman with a beamer. When he and Alexander warned him against resorting to such deliveries, Gilchrist replied that no one could stop him from bowling how he wanted to bowl.

The legitimacy of Gilchrist's bowling now became a source of repeated discussion between captain and manager. Alexander maintained that Gilchrist threw and felt guilty about bowling him; Gaskin agreed that his action was suspect, but told Alexander that the umpires should be the final arbiters of his bowling.

After Gilchrist had bowled a beamer to Pankaj Roy in the first Test, he was asked to appear before the tour committee that evening. Following his admission that he bowled the beamer with the intention of hitting the batsman, he was banned from employing that delivery. It was too dangerous.

It was an edict that Gilchrist didn't challenge, much as he disliked it. Convinced that he was breaking no law and that his beamers were designed to intimidate not to injure, he thought that any Test batsman worth his salt should be able to cope with such a delivery.

The simmering tension between Gilchrist and Alexander exploded at practice before the second Test in an incident involving Basil Butcher. Before this, Butcher and Gilchrist had fallen out over off-the-field matters. Warned that India and Pakistan presented few opportunities for socialising compared to touring England, Gilchrist had bought a large record player and a number of long-playing records to provide entertainment for the team. His generosity was much appreciated by the team who used to gather in the room he shared with Hall to enjoy the music. Because the equipment was heavy, Gilchrist asked that everyone took their turn in carrying it around on their travels, a request to which everyone complied except the solitary Butcher. His repeated refusal to oblige so infuriated Gilchrist that he eventually sold the record player and records, an act of impulsiveness which upset his team-mates, a number of whom blamed him rather than Butcher for their loss.

The latter recalled the fielding practice, 'I had twisted my knee in the first Test at Bombay and had to pass a fitness test to play in the second Test at Kanpur. During one of our practice sessions captain Gerry Alexander was hitting the ball, and one hit came near to me causing me to jump out of the way. Someone chased the ball and Gilly, who was next to me, said, "Butch, if that ball had hit your leg, we would have a big laugh."'

Berated by Gilchrist for always dropping the ball and his refusal to apologise to the bowler, Butcher responded and exchanged angry words with him. As the argument became increasingly heated, Alexander took exception to Gilchrist's coarse language and asked him to apologise. Gilchrist, who thought Alexander too protective of Butcher, refused and let fly with some profanities at his captain before storming off to the pavilion, ignoring his order to return.

When Alexander reported the altercation to Gaskin on his return to the team hotel, Gaskin asked Gilchrist to appear before the tour committee to explain his conduct. Gilchrist denied the use of bad language and his indiscipline, at which point Gaskin called in those team members present at the practice as witnesses. All of them in Gilchrist's presence substantiated Alexander's version of events.

Once the witnesses had left the room, Gaskin asked Gilchrist to apologise, firstly, for calling the captain a liar, secondly, for using abusive language and, thirdly, for leaving the practice without permission. He also told him that as a disciplinary measure he would miss the Kanpur Test and wouldn't play again until he apologised.

Gilchrist refused to comply with Gaskin's request and threatened to boycott the rest of the tour if he was omitted from the Kanpur Test.

Asked by the manager to leave the room to consider the implications of his statement, Gilchrist remained defiant on his return, whereupon Gaskin informed him that he would send him home and he would ask the WICBC for a replacement, a comment that provoked Gilchrist to a further tirade of abuse.

While the necessary arrangements were being made, a delegation of younger players, led by Hunte, Hendriks and Hall, approached the tour committee to plead Gilchrist's case. They said that he was contrite and they asked that, in the interests of his wife, his career and the team, he should be given another chance. Gilchrist himself then appeared and not only tearfully apologised to Alexander and the committee – he would cry very easily when agitated – but also assured them that he would mend his ways.

After deliberating for another hour, the committee reluctantly reinstated Gilchrist, while resolving to disclose the full facts of his misconduct in the management's end-of-tour report, alongside a possible recommendation that he should not represent his country again. He was also omitted from the second Test which cost him his match fee of £30, a hefty sum he could ill afford to lose given that his tour fee outside Tests was a mere £7 a week.

Despite Gilchrist's omission, he still played a part in West Indies' win by 203 runs. Observing Hall's struggle coming to terms with a sluggish matting wicket as India threatened to gain a substantial first-innings lead, he advised him at tea on the second day to bowl a fuller length, advice which Hall instantly heeded, enabling him to go on to take 11 wickets in the match. Yet not everyone was impressed. On the bus back to the hotel at the end of the third day's play, manager Gaskin excoriated Hall for bowling a beamer and injuring the batsman, Manohar Hardikar. While Hall explained it was an accident, Gilchrist weighed in, declaring that the batsman had accepted an apology before lambasting Gaskin for his failure to compliment Hall on his five first-innings wickets.

Still aggrieved about his omission, Gilchrist was in a sullen mood before the start of the game against an Indian Universities XI at Nagpur, telling Hall that Alexander would give him the more favoured end. Hall dismissed such talk but when Alexander duly favoured him, an incensed Gilchrist unleashed a fearsome onslaught on the students, hitting a couple of them with ferocious bouncers. Calling it the most uncompromising bowling he'd ever seen, Hall told Gilchrist to calm down but he was in no mood to listen, taking 6-16 as the home side were shot out for 49. 'I was barely 17 when I was thrown to the lions there,' recalled Farokh Engineer, the renowned Indian wicketkeeper-batsman who was making his first-class debut. 'The mayor of Nagpur in his wisdom said, "Tomorrow, the West Indians are going to face a better team than the Indian team." We were 29 all out [sic]'. Alluding to the terror and destruction wrought by Gilchrist on his team-mates, he recalled the reluctance of their number 11 to face him. 'When Gilchrist comes in to bowl, he starts sliding towards the square-leg umpire and bounced him there. He put his bat up and the ball went over him. Of course, the umpire's shouting "Wide ball, wide ball." And he has to bowl another ball. So everyone was ready to face the next ball except our number 11. He was last seen scampering up the pavilion. "Nahin sub theek hai," he said. "That was a perfect valid delivery."'

Gilchrist took another seven wickets in the victory against Bihar Governor's XI, forcing batsman S.N. Kuckreja to retire hurt in both innings, but he abused vice-captain and fellow Jamaican John Holt junior merely because Holt told him it was improper to bowl bouncers at the lower order.

He resumed his lethal partnership with Hall in the third Test at Calcutta in which West Indies declared at 614/5 before routing India for 124 and 154. At the beginning of India's second innings, the renowned Indian commentator Beri Sarbadhikari pronounced excitedly, 'And in comes Gilchrist, the fastest bowler in all the world, to Contractor and he is bowled,' before describing the flying stumps on the way back to Alexander. Only Vijay Manjrekar, with a plucky 58 not out, provided any real resistance as Gilchrist blew away the tail, taking all five wickets to fall on the final day – four of them clean bowled – to give him match figures of 9-73. His bowling left a lasting impression on Suresh Menon, the celebrated Indian cricket writer. He later recalled 'the terror of watching Roy Gilchrist and Wesley Hall running up to bowl, an umbrella field of bright crimson caps crouching behind the hapless batsmen, who could but bend and weave as he tried to fend off the ball, only to have a gully or short leg fielder throw themselves forward, roll on the ground and come up with the catch. Sitting in the stands among the thousands of grown-up compatriots, I knew that day that even at Eden Gardens, we were still a long way from playing cricket as it was actually played.'

In fact, Gilchrist was by no means at his quickest. Confronted with a green wicket aimed at blunting their pace, he and Hall adjusted their tactics. He later wrote, 'My secret for success was simply this: the Indians did not think we had the common sense to adapt our bowling to any wicket other than a very fast one. They were wrong, dead wrong. I dropped my pace to medium, and let the atmosphere help me – and then helped myself to a few more of the Indian scalps. I have learned a lot in league cricket, and I know that it is no use bowling flat out on a green wicket. I know eight men who will agree with me that medium-pace stuff is a killer – the eight men I sent back in the Calcutta Test.'

He returned to full velocity against South Zone at Bangalore with match figures of 10-117 as the tourists won by 278 runs. He also hit A.S. Krishnaswamy repeatedly in the second innings, one ball hitting his chest and speeding off to the boundary, but the batsman, oozing defiance, went on to score 57.

India's defeat at Calcutta left their cricket in tatters. Their captain Ghulam Ahmed, lacking the confidence of his players, retired immediately and his successor Umrigar resigned on the morning of the fourth Test – although he still played – following a difference of opinion with the selectors over the composition of the team. The selectors now sent for the veteran Vinoo Mankad to captain his country at Madras. He was India's most successful bowler in West Indies' first innings of 500, but he proved less impressive with the bat. Never comfortable against the short ball, he opened his account by steering Gilchrist for four. Gilchrist duly responded, as he later wrote: 'I gave Mankad a real dirty look, and I saw him out of the corner of my eye, talking to the slips and smiling a bit. I know that Mankad was trying to "read" me, and what he "read" was a six-letter word – *bumper*. So, I started off my run from twenty-two yards and all the while as I came in at him, I saw Mankad drifting, drifting, drifting towards the leg slip to keep out of the way of that bumper he was so sure was coming. And all the time I kept getting a better view of those lovely three stumps with no one in front. So I just let that off peg have it like a bomb and sent it flying into the slips. And that was the end of Vinoo Mankad. And his mind-reading!'

Despite gaining a lead of 278, Alexander chose not to enforce the follow-on for reasons that later became clear. He declared at 168/5, setting India 447 to win in just over seven hours. Hall and Gilchrist broke through early and only Borde with 56 showed any defiance in his side's 295-run defeat. The numerous blows he received helped fuel Indian resentment of West Indian 'terror tactics' – as described by commentator Dr P.S. Subbarayan, the transport minister and former president of the BCCI. When Gilchrist struck G.S. Ramchand on the head in the first innings, the large crowd roared and stamped in anger; and on being taunted by A.G. Kripal Singh after he'd hit him for three boundaries, Gilchrist deliberately overstepped the mark and bounced Kripal from a distance of 18 yards, dislodging his turban in the process. Yet, according to the *Times of India* cricket correspondent, the criticism was misplaced. 'There is so much prejudice against the bumper and so much informed opinion about what constitutes one that one can readily understand the derisive boos and jeers that greeted Hall and Gilchrist. Let it be clearly understood that at no time did the West Indies send down more bumpers than they could have legitimately employed – a bumper is a legitimate weapon – and the ball that flattened Ramchand was not a bumper. The batsman misjudged the ball and ducked into it. He had only himself to blame.'

Following yet another humiliation, Mankad was replaced as captain by the 39-year-old Lt. Col. Hemu Adhikari, who was summoned from his military duties to inject a touch of steel into the Indian spine. Batting first in the final Test at Delhi, the home side had their best start in the rubber and Adhikari, with a fighting 63, and Borde rallied the crowd as they flayed Gilchrist to all parts, making him look mortal for the first time in the series. Benefiting from the help given him in playing the short ball by revered Indian coach Kamal Bhandarkar, Borde hit his maiden Test century, but India's total of 415 was eclipsed by the West Indies who, inspired by centuries from Holt, Smith and Solomon, declared at 644/8, a lead of 229.

With Hall and Eric Atkinson both injured, their chances of bowling out India on a flat wicket seemed remote, but with Umrigar and Manjrekar, his arm broken by Gilchrist in the first innings, both unlikely to bat, they seemed doomed once again at 135/3 before another century stand between Borde and Adhikari restored hope. When Gilchrist bowled last man Desai with a couple of overs to go, the home side were 45 runs in front and the match saved, leaving Borde stranded on 96. As the players began to troop off, Adhikari gestured to them to stay put and Manjrekar, his arm heavily plastered, appeared to a rousing reception so as to give Borde the chance to score a second century. Gilchrist went easy on Manjrekar but with Borde it was a different matter. Convinced that he should have been given out caught behind in the 60s, he continued to bowl aggressively and having hit him in the chest with a fiery bumper, he then bowled him another one, which he hooked for four but, to a thousand moans, he upset his stumps in the process. 'Thus it was a bouncer which ended the series,' commented *The Hindu*'s S.K. Gurunathan. 'It has been the most controversial ball since it came to be bowled by Larwood back in 1932. It has also been the wicket-taking ball-in-chief on every ground and in every clime. It made all the difference between India and West Indies in this series.'

India's drubbing and the deterioration of its cricket was raised in the lower house of the Indian parliament by Communist Party deputy T.B. Vittal Rao. After a lively debate in which many members attributed this decline to political meddling, Surjit Singh Majithia, deputy defence minister and former president of the Board of Control for Cricket in India (BCCI), denied their claims. The Indian team weren't that inferior to the West Indies, he said, rather unconvincingly; they simply weren't used to facing someone of Gilchrist's speed and ability.

With his volatile character and disdain for authority, Gilchrist continued to live life on the edge. He ridiculed Alexander's instruction that he tell everyone that his absence from the second Test was due to a pulled muscle, saying he'd never pulled a muscle in his life, and he upset his plans to enforce the follow-on in the fourth Test by refusing to bowl flat out, given that the rubber was already won, insubordination that led to an almighty row with his captain. There was further trouble in the fifth Test when Alexander objected to Gilchrist's noise in the dressing room, telling him to quieten down, a reprimand that Gilchrist deeply resented. He wrote, 'I felt I could have said a lot of things at the top of my voice, too, but did not want any more trouble, so I just dried up inside and let things ride. But deep down, I was wild. Alexander, I felt, had treated me like a schoolma'am treats a first-term boy, and I was certainly no first-term boy.' According to Hall, Gilchrist, with definite views on everyone and everything, thought Alexander was speaking down to him. 'They all tried to convince him differently but he wouldn't budge an inch.' Gilchrist didn't take too much notice of what people told him, recalled Sobers. 'He thought people were laughing at him, which made him even madder.'

Now in the final game in India – against North Zone on a sporting wicket at Amritsar – he met his Waterloo. The fuse was lit by the pre-match comments of captain Swaranjit Singh, an aristocratic Sikh who played with Alexander in the Cambridge XI. Unimpressed with his non-selection in the recent series and the performance of the Indian batting against the West Indian pace attack, he bragged publicly that he could handle Gilchrist and would dispatch him to all parts. According to Sobers, before a ball was bowled, Gilchrist was warned by Alexander to be careful and not to let Singh's comments rile him.

Singh's words lacked conviction when he was bowled by Gilchrist for 1 in North Zone's paltry total of 59, giving the tourists a narrow lead of 17 on first innings.

Set an improbable 246 to win, North Zone were soon in trouble against Gilchrist, who was bowling at his fastest, before Swaranjit halted the slide. Sporting a bright blue turban, he'd scored 26 when he faced Gilchrist in the final session on the second day. (Gilchrist in his autobiography mistakenly refers to it as the final over before lunch on the third day.) Having begun with a bouncer, Gilchrist then bowled an overpitched yorker which

Swaranjit drove straight back for four: as he passed the bowler he said, 'You like that one? Beautiful, wasn't it?' Incensed by the taunt, Gilchrist then bowled a beamer straight at the batsman's head, just about the fastest ball he ever bowled in his life, asking him, 'How do you like that lovely beamer?'

'Now Mr Singh did not seem to like that beamer any more than I had liked that four he had scored,' Gilchrist later wrote. 'Neither did our skipper. But I thought it was great, just great.'

He then followed it with a short ball which Swaranjit pushed to short leg, where Alexander dropped it.

Unhappy with his reprieve, Gilchrist resorted to another beamer which so unnerved Swaranjit that he turned to Alexander and said, 'Gerry, are you going to make this happen? This man is out to kill me.' Alexander then spoke to Gilchrist and told him to 'cut it out' and when Gilchrist responded with another head-high beamer, his fate was sealed. He was immediately taken off and as they left the field at close of play Alexander informed Gilchrist that he'd bowled his last ball of the game. Gilchrist asked Alexander if he could at least finish the match, even if he didn't bowl, but his captain replied that he'd made up his mind and that was that. 'I found it impossible to lead Gilchrist; and I saw no other way if discipline was to be maintained,' he later wrote in his captain's tour report.

'I had no qualms whatsoever about the decision. Further, his bowling action is entirely suspect. In my opinion he does throw.'

Alexander's resolve to send Gilchrist home was endorsed by the tour committee, who'd been urged by the WICBC to brook no nonsense from him. Manager Berkeley Gaskin was a kind man who went out of his way to encourage the younger players. He'd advocated clemency for Gilchrist over his outburst at Kanpur, but as the tour had progressed his patience had worn thin with Gilchrist's persistent disrespect towards Alexander. Fully aware that he had been placed in the spotlight as the first black man to manage West Indies on tour, Gaskin was determined to live up to expectation by restoring discipline after the disastrous England tour the previous year, which meant grasping the Gilchrist nettle.

Gaskin's opinion was fully supported by vice-captain Holt, who'd felt the full force of Gilchrist's tongue on occasions, and Ramadhin. Although the latter had attended Gilchrist's wedding the previous year, the two weren't close, a situation exacerbated by Gilchrist's tendency to deprecate Ramadhin's bowling in a series in which the latter had been dropped.

Bolstered by the support of the tour committee, Alexander summoned his errant fast bowler and said, 'Gilchrist, you don't go to Pakistan. You leave by the next plane for home. Good afternoon.'

'That shook me,' Gilchrist wrote. 'I did not feel angry, not even hurt, just ashamed that I had let West Indian cricket down. When we West Indians go on tour, we are always careful to keep our good name. We aim at being the best sportsmen in the world, and I guess Alexander and some of the other committee men felt I just had not been one of the best sportsmen.'

Resigned to his fate, Gilchrist went to his room and stayed there, while others, led by Hunte, Kanhai and Hall, sympathised with his plight. Although conscious that he was a smouldering volcano that could erupt at any moment, many of the players liked and respected Gilchrist. Aside from the shrewd advice he dispensed to his fellow bowlers, he could be good company off the field: kind, generous and witty, valuable attributes on a long tour in an alien environment. His bullish self-confidence also raised morale, while his unrelenting efforts in the most arduous of conditions elicited great admiration. Even his foibles were treated with greater indulgence than would be the norm on account of his difficult upbringing. According to Hall, Gilchrist's outsider status within the West Indies team and the feeling that he wasn't valued probably contributed to his aggressive behaviour. 'What the young boy missed in the school room, he made up for by outclassing everyone in the streets where he played cricket. Cricket brought out the best and the worst of him. Gilly knew the game; he really understood cricket, and of course, he excelled at bowling. His cricket knowledge was immense, yet he was rarely heeded; that was difficult for him to accept. Underneath the bravado, Gilchrist hid his insecurity, but he had no knowledge of how to leave his past behind.'

Later that evening a delegation approached Alexander, who was playing bridge with Sobers, Hendriks and Willy Rodriguez in the captain's room, to reconsider his decision and give Gilchrist one more chance. According to Hendriks, Alexander put down his cards and said, 'Gentlemen, it's an easy solution you know, it is either him or me, make up your mind.' Then he picked up his cards and resumed the game.

Gilchrist's farewell to his team-mates greatly upset him. Hall later wrote, 'I went in last with the other fellows already on the coach to Pakistan, and found him sitting with tears trickling down his face. All he could say, over and over again, was "The only thing that really hurts me is when I remember how hard I bowled."'

A couple of days later Gilchrist refused to pose for a photograph in his touring tie before beginning his long journey back to England, while his team-mates proceeded to Pakistan. When passing through Delhi to get the train to Bombay, he told the hordes of reporters, 'I don't want to say nothing, man,' only then to open up. He accepted that he'd disregarded Alexander's instructions not to bowl beamers, but maintained that he wasn't bound by such instructions as bowling beamers to scare the batsman, as opposed to hitting them, was every fast bowler's prerogative.

'If a fast bowler really wanted to hurt a batsman, he could well do that by employing more effective means.

'For instance, no one can prevent me from violating the no-ball rule and hurling a real fizzer at the batsman.'

As the train departed, he said with a smile, 'I don't know why I'm being sent back.' On arrival at Bombay airport, he refused to sign autographs but remarked, 'I'm going home happy with joy. I'm not frightened.'

In Gilchrist's absence, West Indies were surprisingly beaten 2-1 in Pakistan, a series marred by faulty umpiring with Sobers, the victim of several contentious decisions, threatening to go home. He later wrote: 'When Gerry saw what the Pakistan umpires were doing to me, he said that he wished he had kept Gilchrist to even the balance. If we had Gilchrist in the side, we would have won the series. If the umpires hadn't given their batsmen out, he would have knocked them out.'

Gilchrist's departure split opinion. 'Much has been said and written by an irresponsible press about Gilchrist and Hall overdoing the use of bumpers and beamers,' wrote the eminent Indian cricket writer Dicky Rutnagur, 'but let it be said that one scarcely saw them bowling beamers after the Kanpur Test in which Hardikar was hit on his left ear by Hall.

'Only those closest to the West Indies team suspected internal ramblings, for on the field Gilchrist was every bit a team man, giving of his best.

'Even the greatest disciplinarian would feel sorry to see such a gallant bowler return home in disgrace. The part he played in the West Indies beating India so convincingly is not completely reflected in the 26 Test wickets on the most unhelpful pitches, and the sub-climatic conditions were not always pleasant.

'Gilchrist toiled for long spells, giving the Indian batsmen no respite or relief. In all his first-class matches – he played in only 12 – Gilchrist captured 71 wickets, which, to the best of my knowledge, is the record for a visiting bowler in India.

'The Indian crowd, misguided by some writers and broadcasters, sometimes booed Gilchrist for his bumpers, but all the same he was a great favourite with them, and the official developments will be followed with great interest in this country.'

There were those, like Butcher, who attributed his fate to the prevalent customs of class and racial difference in Jamaica at that time and to Alexander's failure to handle him properly. 'But we were hurt because, at the time, we all regarded Gilly as the best fast bowler in the world. For someone to be regarded as the best in the world to be belittled for what I thought was no reason at all was inexcusable.'

Kanhai called Gilchrist's downfall the greatest waste of cricket talent. He wasn't always the villain portrayed in India. 'The trouble with Gilly is that he attracts trouble like honey attracts a bee ... I reckon a few individuals ruined Gilly on that tour.' Underneath the fireball was 'a real nice guy if he took to you'. 'Somehow you never hear the tales of the fellows he's helped with a few words of advice and encouragement.'

On the other hand, Hendriks, a good friend of Alexander's, disagreed vehemently that the captain had acted unfairly. 'I really can't say there was anything else that could have been done. He could have gone home after the second Test match.'

His view was supported by Sobers in *20 Years at the Top*. 'The beamer is cricket's deadliest delivery, because when aimed at the batsman it is hard to pick up and harder still to avoid. It is rightly banned, and any bowler bowling it deliberately cannot expect to have a long career.

'Many bowlers have let slip a beamer in their time and have usually apologised to the batsman … But Gilly rarely said sorry: he meant it.

'Gerry Alexander had also been to Cambridge University, and beamers weren't part of his cricketing philosophy. He was a highly strung, tense man who smoked up to 40 cigarettes a day. He was always urging the players to greater efforts. … He soon fell out with Gilly who, though capable of showing a fair amount of common sense on occasions, did not take too much notice of what people told him. He thought people were laughing at him which made him even madder. When Alexander told him to stop bowling beamers he ignored him.

'It was a difficult situation for the captain. His best fast bowler wasn't carrying out his instructions. Discipline was stricter in those days, and Alexander decided that Gilchrist would have to go.'

'Gerry was a terrific disciplinarian,' recalled Rodriguez, a white Trinidadian. 'Gilly also had other problems and just did not have the intelligence to understand what was going on.'

During a break in London on his return home, manager Berkeley Gaskin told Baz Freckleton, the sports editor of Jamaica's *The Star*, that the deterioration in the relationship between

Gilchrist and Alexander had reached such a nadir that, in the interest of the reputation of West Indies and the morale of the team, the former had to be sent home.

Having committed earlier offences that could well have seen him banished, he persistently flouted Alexander's authority on and off the field, of which bowling beamers against instructions was but the final straw. Gaskin admitted Gilchrist would have been a considerable asset in Pakistan, but his inclusion might certainly have wrecked the tour. 'Ever since I've been associated with the game, either as a player or administrator, I have always insisted on discipline. ... To me, discipline, sportsmanship, loyalty and respect for constituted authority are still ideals that must be retained at all cost in West Indies cricket even it means sending home the best player.'

As for Alexander, aside from some brief remarks on his arrival back in the West Indies, he never publicly commented on his rift with Gilchrist, but he wrote in his tour report that Gilchrist was 'completely illiterate' and 'had maniacal tendencies'. 'It was difficult to make him understand much of what was required of him and instead he hid behind persecution and inferiority complexes.'

Knowing his background, he and Gaskin tried to cut away the rougher edges, making him more tolerant of his team-mates and more sympathetic to the spirit of the game. 'In this respect we put up with more than we would have tolerated from any other member of the side.'

Alexander also confided to Chester Watson that Gilchrist's temper and intransigence were the main causes of his downfall. He simply wouldn't cooperate. According to Watson, the clash wasn't one of race and class but of personality. 'Gerry was a good person for cricket and the team. If Gilly had been more discerning, he could have been guided by Gerry.'

Even Gilchrist came to accept that Alexander, a tough, honourable leader charged with restoring discipline after the 1957 tour of England, had acted justifiably (although his view fluctuated on this issue). 'But Conrad and Co. couldn't get Gerry Alexander to change his mind, and I guess now he was right. Being a tour captain is not a child's job; a skipper has to be tough when it comes to discipline, and Alexander was just that when it came to my case. And I suppose now, on reflection, that it served me right.'

The last word should be left to Michael Manley, the socialist prime minister of Jamaica between 1972 and 1980. He wrote in *A History of West Indies Cricket*, 'In the final analysis Gilchrist had only himself to blame, however much there is a larger sense in which the fate that befell him must be seen in the context of an entire social system. His departure was a tragedy born of the interaction between a flawed individual and a malformed society; an angry misfit and a too slowly evolving system of authority. Those who knew Gilchrist and the society of which he was a product could detect an almost Greek inevitability as man and system proceeded to their inevitable and final collision.'

Chapter 5

Halcyon Days at Middleton

IN 1958 Gilchrist joined the Central Lancashire League (CLL) making his home in England for the next 28 years, during which time he played for 12 different clubs. It wasn't unusual for professionals to move around and go where the money was, but the fact that he was so nomadic says something about his volatile personality and his various clashes with authority.

The CLL lived in the shadow of the Lancashire League, but, along with the latter and the Bradford League, it provided very strong competition. Founded in 1892, its 15 clubs, based mainly to the east of Manchester, played each other home and away each season with no time or overs limit. Although the 1950s witnessed a marked decline in attendances as greater leisure opportunities became available, the leagues still generated considerable interest among these tight-knit communities, especially when international cricketers were on display.

Each CLL and Lancashire League side was permitted one professional whose value would be measured not only by his own performance, and that of the team, but also by the way he could motivate his team-mates and the local community. Because many professionals commanded a greater income for their weekend appearances than most county players received for a six-day week, there was little problem in attracting top players to the leagues, not least from the West Indies, where making a living from the game proved all but impossible.

Their pioneer was undoubtedly Learie Constantine, who overcame ignorance and racial prejudice during his time at the Lancashire League club Nelson between 1929 and 1937. An all-rounder of flamboyant brilliance, his exploits on the field made him a great box-office attraction wherever he played and helped Nelson to seven championships, while his magnetic personality off it soon won him the affection of the entire community. Constantine in turn became devoted to Nelson, living there for 20 years, and helping to forge a special relationship between Lancashire and the Caribbean. During the 1930s, fellow West Indians such as George Headley, Ellis Achong and Manny Martindale followed Constantine into the Lancashire League, while the success of the West Indies in England in 1950 accelerated that trend: Clyde Walcott at Enfield, Everton Weekes at Bacup and Frank Worrell at Radcliffe – in the CLL – led the way, followed in 1958 by Collie Smith (Burnley), Conrad Hunte (Enfield) and Alf Valentine (Rishton).

With the opportunity to make some money for the first time in his life, it was hardly surprising that Gilchrist was attracted by the lure of league cricket. In July 1957 he seemed destined to join Colne in the Lancashire League, only for the committee to reject him on the grounds that he wasn't good enough.

As Colne closed one door, Middleton of the CLL opened another. Shunning their traditional reliance on home-grown products such as Hedley Verity, one of England's finest spinners, and Frank Tyson, the destroyer of Australia in 1954/55 with his exceptional pace, they approached Gilchrist during the Headingley Test. He accepted in principle, subject to him consulting Worrell. Once Worrell had assured him that Middleton was the right club for him, Gilchrist signed a two-year contract worth £750 (equal to around £14,000 in 2023) a year, plus £250 expenses, a princely sum in those days. With Sobers signing for Radcliffe that year and Hanif Mohammad for Crompton, joining other eminent professionals such as the Australian Cec Pepper and Indian all-rounder Vinoo Mankad, the CLL was doing all it could to win back the crowds.

Buoyed by his new-found status following his success against Pakistan, Gilchrist arrived at Middleton in April 1958 to be met by a three-man welcoming committee at the station. He was taken to a golf club for lunch and photographed for the local paper, looking most demure, in the company of club chairman Alderman T. Heywood. Weeks later the cricket club attended its first civic reception in the form of an official welcome to Gilchrist, the mayor of Middleton, Joseph Britton, telling him that the town wanted to reach out to him and let him know he was among friends. 'You are already getting a warm place in our hearts,' he declared, to which Gilchrist, replying through Middleton's wicketkeeper Alf Barlow, expressed his gratitude for all the generosity shown him.

One small boil that needed to be lanced related to his accommodation. Unhappy with his £5-a-week lodgings on the Langley Estate, sharing with a fellow West Indian and keen to have his own home, especially with marriage looming, he threatened to tear up his contract unless the club found him a house. It was at this point that Alf Barlow, landlord of the local pub, discovered a 100-year-old cottage owned by the local brewery. The club thought it too dilapidated, but Gilchrist said it was fine and, along with his team-mates, he was soon on his knees helping workmen scrub it out before it was decorated and furnished at the club's expense. Before the arrival of Gilchrist's fiancée, Barlow gave him dinner at the pub, which was conveniently located next to the cricket ground, so that he was never short of company in the evening.

On 25 April 1958, Gilchrist made his debut for Middleton against Crompton in a game that will live long in the memory. In reply to Middleton's 141/9 declared, and in front of a quiet, tense crowd at their Glebe Street ground, Crompton professional Hanif Mohammad and his opening partner Wilf Sutcliffe negotiated Gilchrist's opening spell with relative ease, putting on 63 for the first wicket. Their only uncomfortable moment came when Sutcliffe held up his hand to stop Gilchrist in mid-run and took a comb out of his pocket to brush his hair. Irked by this gratuitous interruption, Gilchrist walked back to the sightscreen, charged in and let go a thunderbolt so fast that the ball was in the wicketkeeper's gloves before Sutcliffe had lifted his bat.

Having conceded 32 from his first six (eight-ball) overs, Gilchrist then switched ends with dramatic results. With the sun and wind at his back and the advantage of a downward slope, he bowled Hanif with a fast full toss before running through the rest of the order, taking all ten wickets in 25 balls, including four in four. Even a brief stoppage for the blinding sun couldn't save Crompton as they succumbed to Gilchrist, who had taken to heart the primary need of a fast bowler in league cricket to bowl accurately, by hitting the stumps eight times. According to Middleton wicketkeeper Trevor Roydes, who stood further back than he'd ever done previously, 'He was the quickest I've ever seen. Tyson used to net at Middleton before going down to Northants, and Gilly was faster than Frank. I was short and had to keep relatively close at 15 yards to take the ball waist-high. It was a lonely time since the slips were always 15 yards behind me! I couldn't afford fillet steaks but inserted plasticine in my right "Arthur McIntyre" glove. I would never have played on Sundays then, my hands were too badly bruised, but in 27 years of keeping I never broke a finger. Gilly was phenomenally fast and nobody fancied him much in the nets either. Bowling flat out at one stump, he once hit it nine times out of ten.'

His performance set the template for an astonishing season in which he captured 137 wickets, but amid his litany of achievements controversy continued to stalk him. Against Littleborough in June, he drew loud protests from the home crowd by repeatedly hitting their veteran opener, former Lancashire player and league professional Les Warburton, now playing as an amateur, on the hand and the body. Twice Warburton walked down the wicket to protest, once after Gilchrist had fielded the ball and thrown it back down the pitch, sending it between the batsman's legs before hitting the wickets. On another occasion Warburton turned to Middleton captain Jimmy Hyde and said, 'This man is throwing. He doesn't play cricket, he makes war,' to which Gilchrist replied to his captain, 'I've got the ball. He got a bat – best man wins.'

After 100 minutes of stoical defence, Warburton was treated to another beamer which went for four byes and a lifter which thudded into his ribs. The next ball he gave his wicket away and departed in high dudgeon. 'I don't mind bumpers but I object to having the ball thrown at me,' he told the local paper. 'Certainly, Gilchrist's speed is a problem in itself,' reported local cricket writer Rex Pogson in *The Cricketer* when alluding to the controversy. 'Lancashire experts consider him the fastest bowler ever to play in the league.'

There were further ructions in the home game against Oldham prior to which Mayor Britton presented Gilchrist with the ball with which he'd taken 10-38 against Crompton, specially mounted and inscribed with a silver plate. In front of a crowd of several thousand, Gilchrist all but emulated his feat of taking all ten wickets, only for the last Oldham batsman to be run out, but in the course of his spell he became embroiled in heated exchanges with Oldham professional Cec Pepper.

Pepper was a temperamental Australian whose feisty personality and withering tongue couldn't conceal a cricketer of the highest quality. Exiled from post-war Australian cricket following an altercation with Don Bradman over an lbw decision, he moved to England to find fame in the leagues. Sensing a soulmate, Gilchrist liked and admired Pepper and was a regular in his Sunday XI teams, but when he deliberately bowled a beamer at Oldham's Bill Lawton that narrowly missed his head, Pepper saw red. 'Throw another of those at any amateur,' he threatened Gilchrist, 'and I'll stuff you with the rough end of a revolving pineapple.'

'You're not fast enough, Pep,' Gilchrist replied.

'I'm bloody deadly from four yards,' he retorted, 'and he can only call "no ball", mate.'

'Gilchrist visibly wilted,' wrote Ken Piesse, Pepper's biographer. 'Pep was not a man to upset.'

The friction continued when Middleton travelled to Rochdale, the championship leaders. Bowling first on a lively pitch, Gilchrist's first ball hit the home side's professional, Indian all-rounder Dattu Phadkar, in the stomach and then his first ball to fellow opener George Holland broke two of his teeth, the ball ricocheting on to his wicket. His continued overuse of the bouncer upset the crowd whose taunts in turn further darkened his mood, but solid half-centuries from Phadkar and his compatriot Kalyan Mitra consigned the match to a dreary draw. 'Gilchrist is a good enough bowler to get wickets without laying on the dramatic stuff,' noted the *Oldham Chronicle*, 'for that is all this West Indian seems to be doing; playing to the gallery. The more he controls his quick reaction to the little things that crop up in a game to annoy a fast bowler, the more use he will be to Middleton and the League.'

Another Indian to get the better of him was Stockport professional Vinoo Mankad when the two teams met. Gilchrist wrote, 'I had 96 wickets under my belt at the time and I was really making the ball fly about a bit when Vinoo decided to tell me a few facts of life. "Gilly," he said kindly to me, "don't you know that professionals always give the other professional a chance to score fifty." Now this was really something new to me and set me rocking on my heels. But I was young and green and I was eager to please the men who knew the ropes. So when Vinoo had got in the eighties I began bowling off-spinners to help him on his way.'

After Mankad made 97 Gilchrist admitted to finishing the match a lot wiser because his Indian opponent had reminded him that he must discard all sentiment if he was to become a successful all-round professional. 'But I got my revenge the next time Vinoo and I met up. I just slaughtered them, and Mankad, clever moves and all, got next to nothing for his pains.'

By now Gilchrist's fiancée, Novlyn Graham, a farmer's daughter from the parish of St Elizabeth whom he met in Kingston, had arrived from Jamaica. Two weeks later they were married at Oldham Registry Office – Gilchrist resplendent in tails, Novlyn in a full-length gown of white Chantilly lace – followed by a reception at their home organised by Alf Barlow.

Alongside officials and team-mates from Middleton, the guests included Frank Worrell, Sonny Ramadhin, Alf Valentine, Collie Smith, Tom Dewdney, Cec Pepper, and two Indian cricketers, Subhash Gupte and Vijay Manjrekar.

With no honeymoon to get in the way of his cricket, Gilchrist continued to cut a swathe through the opposition, returning figures of 8-27 against Royton, 8-17 against Milnrow and 8-18 against Littleborough, ensuring that Middleton were champions for the first time in 20 years. Asked to lead the team off the field after his demolition of Littleborough, Gilchrist appeared indifferent to the acclaim from the large crowd but deep down he felt a real sense of pride. Thanks to the efforts of captain Jimmy Hyde, who'd gone out of his way to help him settle, he'd won the confidence of his team-mates and appreciated being part of a happy outfit.

Declaring Middleton to be worthy winners of the CLL, Rex Pogson wrote that Gilchrist's speed, even when the wickets were soft, left almost everyone without an answer. 'There were protests that he was intimidating and bowled too many bumpers, but the figures show that a large percentage of his wickets were clean bowled. In his first match he took all ten wickets, once he took nine and four times eight. Twice he had four wickets in consecutive balls and there was also a hat-trick.'

He'd also gained the esteem of the local community who revelled in his exploits, and his presence boosted attendances across Lancashire. After he'd played at Nelson in a friendly against Pudsey Britannia, the cricket journalist Noel Wild wrote, 'Gilchrist – and it is no surprise to me – has shown that public interest is not dead. Those who did turn up went to see Gilchrist. And he did not let them down. He took 7-35, hit the wicket five times and now and then cartwheeled the stumps out of the ground, and in his tenth to 13th overs took four wickets for no runs. I was not present. But my colleague Eric Greenwood reports that the crowd rose to Gilchrist. He electrified Seedhill. And certainly, I have not known a cricketer infect public conversation in Nelson (or Colne) so much since Pat Crawford stood the crowd on its ear in 1955.

'Gilchrist is as controversial as Crawford was and is a better bowler to boot. He has the "mean streak" in him like Crawford. He is faster than Crawford, and if anything, even more hostile; he plays the game hard; and he has the sense to get the ball up and on the wicket for League batsmen.

'I don't know what the Middleton crowds are like, but I saw him at Rochdale three weeks ago, and, as I wrote then, he would certainly draw the crowds here.'

According to John Kay, the cricket correspondent of the *Manchester Evening News,* Gilchrist was as much sinned against as sinning. There was evidence to suggest that opposition captains had been encouraged to produce sensational Sunday headlines. Alluding to his tally of 137 wickets, 110 of which were bowled, Kay wrote, 'This is a performance of great cricketing merit yet I seldom saw it advanced in Gilchrist's favour. He was always accused of being a dangerous bowler, one who was always dropping the ball short or zooming it through the air head high.'

Although contracted to Middleton for another year, Gilchrist was already looking further afield. There was talk of him going to Nelson, but they couldn't afford his terms of £1,400 a year, and after playing for Bacup as a sub-pro, and taking 7-26 against East Lancashire in their last match in 1958, he subsequently signed for the club for the 1960 season. His contract was worth £900 a year, plus £250 expenses, and was said to be one of the highest ever in the Lancashire League. His desire to move clubs was hastened by the negative headlines he attracted, not least doubts about his action and hostile crowds at away fixtures.

On Gilchrist's recommendation, Crompton had signed fast bowler Cec Wright, who'd played once for Jamaica against Barbados, as their professional for 1959. Wright, who enjoyed living with the Gilchrists that season, struggled at first in alien conditions and was reprimanded by his club for turning up late to a cup match at Littleborough. Having missed the team bus, Wright went to watch Gilchrist play at Middleton and when Gilchrist saw him, he told him to get a taxi to the ground immediately.

Despite his close friendship with Gilchrist, Wright was shown little mercy when Middleton played Crompton. Coming in to bat against Gilchrist, he was hit three times on the thigh. 'At the end of the over Gilly came down to me,' Wright later recalled. 'He had his cap in his hand. He gave it to me and says, "Put that in your front pocket, Cec. Next time I hit you on the thigh it will cushion the blow."'

Following a discussion with Worrell, Wright learned to bowl a fuller length and prospered, becoming in time a legend of the Lancashire leagues. Settling in Royton and marrying a local girl, he continued to shine for Uppermill second XI in his dotage before retiring in 2019 at the age of 85 with more than 7,000 wickets to his name.

Gilchrist's premature departure from India provided a disturbing backdrop to the 1959 league season when his bowling and conduct increasingly came under critical scrutiny. According to Rishton professional John Rutherford, unless the umpires took a firmer stance against intimidatory bowling, league cricket could descend into a bloodbath, while to fellow Australian Bobby Simpson, the professional at Accrington, whose thumb was injured by Gilchrist in a friendly, the West Indian flouted the spirit of the game. He wrote, 'I would rank Gilchrist as fast as any bowler I have played against and that includes Lindwall, Miller, Heine, Tyson, Statham, Trueman, Adcock, Rorke and Meckiff.

'A fast bowler has to use his gifts within reason, but Gilchrist broke two unwritten laws in two matches I saw. Firstly, he bowled many bumpers at tailenders; secondly, he overdid the beam ball.'

More provocatively, Lowerhouse professional Bob Bartels called him a killer in front of the Indian touring team in the dressing rooms at Old Trafford, and when Gilchrist replied, 'What's the matter? Have I murdered your mother?', Bartels left immediately.

Ironically enough, it was while deputising for the injured Simpson in Accrington's game against Rishton in the Worsley Cup, the knockout competition of the Lancashire League, that Gilchrist further sullied his reputation. Having rattled Rutherford with some nasty short stuff as soon as he came in, the Australian came down the wicket to him and said, 'It would be nice to have some practice for my tour,' a request which Gilchrist predictably refused. Resorting to type, he was no-balled twice by the umpires for throwing. Claiming that he'd bowled all over the world without ever being called, Gilchrist vehemently protested his innocence to the umpires, an altercation that became increasingly fractious, so much so that when the batsmen vented their opinions, he resorted to a plethora of bumpers that outraged Rishton's supporters. 'Whatever one may think of all this the fact remains that Roy Gilchrist is proving a great draw to the crowds,' wrote the cricket correspondent of the *Civil and Military Gazette*, a daily English-language newspaper published in Lahore. 'The takings for the Worsley Cup match were the biggest for years. The crowds go to see the innocents slaughtered. There is also the attraction of possible "incidents" which follow Gilchrist around like a shadow.'

Controversy aside, Gilchrist picked up where he left off the previous season, with seven cheap wickets against Ashton, hitting all three stumps in one over, and another seven against Milnrow, a game in which he clashed with opener Ken Leach, who'd batted doggedly for 78. During the closing stages of their innings, Gilchrist bowled him a beamer which went for four byes. Leach then mis-hooked a bouncer and as he scurried a single, Gilchrist bounded up the wicket to take the catch. They collided, Leach's bat accidentally striking Gilchrist's leg, and he was run out. As he made his way back to the pavilion, his protests at the decision were stifled when Gilchrist approached him aggressively, gesticulating towards his trouser leg, and brandishing a fist before the batsman walked off.

One ball later, after taking the final wicket, Gilchrist alleged that Leach had deliberately hit him on the leg with his bat. To prove the blow, he showed Middleton officials the broken skin on his right leg.

Having endured crowd hostility at Oldham in the Wood Cup, the knockout competition of the CLL, Gilchrist suffered a similar fate at Radcliffe, where a minority of the record crowd began jeering him as soon as he stepped on to the field. Calling their disrespect towards him childish, the *Middleton Guardian* wrote, 'Obviously his quite undeserved reputation as a dangerous bowler had gone before him. His bowling brilliance went unapplauded. Instead, he was subjected to persistent barracking, especially when

Radcliffe batsman, David Ogden, was hit twice by the ball and laid out on the turf.' Claiming that both balls had been pitched up, the reporter quoted one Middleton supporter telling a protesting Radcliffe fan, 'Well, he's got a bat, hasn't he?'

Regretting this departure from the traditional high standards of the CLL and the taunting of Gilchrist at various grounds, the *Oldham Chronicle* wondered whether it was a form of gamesmanship by the crowds.

Days after this skirmish the WICBC announced that Gilchrist wouldn't be considered for selection against MCC that winter. Upset by his omission and with the general hostility he'd faced that summer, he put his side of the story in an article in *The Gleaner*.

'I am barracked and booed wherever I play. I have even had rows with them but I have never let it worry me: I let the other fellow do the worrying.

'I don't argue with my fellow professionals. If they insult me, I save my reply until I meet them on the field. It is then, with a ball in my hand, that I can give them my most effective answer.

'Cricket arguments should be settled on the field. That's my view. I show no mercy and expect none in return. Other professionals don't like me because I bowl all out. If they're nearing 50 and a fat collection from fans, I bowl all the harder.

'Nobody can expect me to soft-pedal. If they ask me to take it easy, I just shorten my run. And that's when I'm most dangerous.

'Cricket is not a baby's game. I give batsmen the lot. I bowl at them, not the wicket. When I'm running up, I see only gleaming white pads, not stumps.'

He couldn't understand the attitude of the crowds. 'Perhaps it is because I treat every batsman alike and bowl bumpers to young amateurs just as I do to seasoned professionals. The No.11 batsman gets the same type of delivery as the No.1.'

He reckoned that if a player wasn't good enough to measure up to the standards of league cricket, he should not be in the side. The second team was the place for him. The bouncer was the only weapon a fast bowler had. If he thought a bouncer would unnerve the batsman or cause him to mishit, he wouldn't hesitate to bowl them, even against friends.

'If I had a young son who wanted to play cricket against me, I could not ease up simply because he was my son. It's not in my nature.

'Hecklers should ask this question: what is the point of clubs engaging Test-class professionals if there are going to be grouses about them running through the opposition?

'If they don't want to play against me, they should be man enough to admit it and tell their clubs.

'And if the clubs that pick them don't think they are good enough, they should leave them out.'

He concluded, 'All I want to do, and all my club wants me to do, is get wickets.

'So far there have been no complaints from Middleton and, let's face it, no other club, simply because Middleton usually provide bumper gates.'

Amid some stunning figures that propelled Middleton to another league title, the rancour continued. Gilchrist was subjected to a slew of bouncers by Werneth's opening bowler and he responded in kind, action which prompted loud barracking from their crowd. He also was taunted by the Rochdale crowd for his 40-yard run-up and for hitting batsman Geoff Frain on the head with a bouncer, the latter's retirement preventing him once again claiming all ten wickets. On top of this, he was severely reprimanded by the CLL at their July meeting following a joint complaint by two umpires for displays of dissent when decisions failed to go his way.

A week later there was further controversy when Crompton's popular professional and fellow West Indian, Doug Clarke, played a ball from Gilchrist back to the bowler, whereupon Gilchrist tried to run him out, the ball just missing Clarke's head. This wanton aggression so antagonised the crowd that loud barracking ensued and the umpires had to ask them to be quiet.

There was also trouble at Oldham. Drawn against them in the Wood Cup, Gilchrist was ridiculed by their supporters as opening batsman Frank Molyneux dispatched him to all parts in his 114 not out, then the highest score by an amateur against him. According to Gordon Ripley, later a respected league umpire, who was watching Gilchrist for the first time, he was frightening to everyone except Molyneux, who played the innings of his life. 'Gilly just couldn't bowl to him and at one point actually bowled a couple of overs of leggies.' He did, however, hit one of the later batsmen, prompting a fresh bout of crowd hostility, so much so that umpire Dave Tolhurst warned them that if they continued to abuse Gilchrist, he would stop the game.

In the league match at Oldham, Gilchrist gained his revenge by having Molyneux caught without scoring, mishooking a bouncer, a dismissal that riled the crowd. He then locked horns with Bill Lawton, husband of the actress Dora Bryan, after he bowled him three successive bouncers and a beamer. Lawton complained to the umpire who had a word with Gilchrist, but Gilchrist then bowled another beamer, whereupon Oldham captain Bob Acton strode on to the field only to be told to get off by his opposite number Jimmy Hyde. At the end of the home side's innings, as Gilchrist made his way to the pavilion, several women called him a killer amid a string of expletives. He ignored the insults but later commented, 'The Central Lancashire crowds mostly just come to sit and watch. Half of them do not know what is going on, and do not want to if their side is losing … The Lancashire League fan is more cricket proud, has a better understanding of things a fellow is trying to do and trying not to do.'

Oldham's three-run win, a result decided by Lawton running out Middleton's Trevor Roydes for backing up at the non-striker's end without giving him a warning, although he'd previously warned one of his team-mates, merely served to inflame relations between the two sides. Oldham claimed that after the game Gilchrist had threatened future retribution to some of their players and they approached the return fixture at Middleton with some foreboding.

After the champions batted first, matters came to a head when Gilchrist hit opener Molyneux on the shoulder, forcing him to retire hurt. He then struck Jack Kimber hard on the knee and felled 17-year-old David Booth with a lifter that struck him in the groin. As the youngster writhed on the ground in agony, his father rushed to the wicket, shouting at Gilchrist, followed by acting captain Lawton, the club professional Harry Broomhead and president Ian Batley. During a heated conversation between Lawton and the Middleton players, Gilchrist stood alone near the sightscreen, waiting to bowl his next delivery. It never came, since Lawton, with the full support of his side and club officials, declared at 21/2, thus conceding the match.

As the players left the field, Gilchrist flicking the ball from hand to hand, the home crowd surged over to the Oldham dressing room to give vent to their displeasure at the abandonment. Arguments broke out among rival groups of supporters, some of which nearly came to blows, with one woman from Oldham shouting, 'You're a lot of silly men. You only came to see Gilchrist hurt someone. Well now he has done. I hope you are satisfied.'

While the mayor of Middleton, S.A. Chisholm, became embroiled in an acrimonious discussion with Oldham officials, a taciturn Gilchrist, wearing a red blazer over his cricket clothes, emerged from the pavilion to be met by back-slapping fans and cheers of, 'Good old Gilly. You've scared them off this time.'

In this fractious atmosphere, the Oldham players stayed in the dressing room for more than half an hour. When they emerged, they were surrounded by a gaggle of home supporters and booed out of the ground to a chorus of 'sissies' and 'softies'. Responding to captain Hyde's allegation that their protest was a pre-arranged publicity stunt – the Oldham players had told him they were going to do this after their previous encounter – and his contention that Gilchrist had bowled perfectly fairly, Oldham president James Batby dismissed his claims as nonsense. 'Of the 23 balls sent down by Gilchrist, eight were bumpers and two were beamers. There might have been a serious accident if Lawton had not intervened.' As for Lawton, he told the local press, 'The umpires are empowered to stop this sort of bowling, but if they do not, someone has to make a protest.' He was convinced that Gilchrist would kill a batsman one day. 'In my view he throws and he is the fastest in the business.'

A few years later Lawton was batting in a second XI match for Sussex against Hampshire on a fast, bouncy wicket at the United Services Ground, Portsmouth, when he was struck a nasty blow in the ribs by Barbadian John Holder, who was genuinely quick. Having slumped to the ground in severe pain, he suddenly leapt to his feet and started calling Holder a hooligan for bowling bouncers at him. 'For five minutes or so, he ranted and raved and no one could stop him as he walked round and round the stumps,' recollected Holder. "I've met your type before," he shouted at me … I waited for an explanation. It came in one word. "Gilchrist".'

Oldham's dramatic protest left Gilchrist shaken and surprised. 'Why, they did not do this sort of thing back in Jamaica, and cricket there can be crazy at times,' he later wrote. That evening he discussed the day's events with Lawton in the pub, but there was little meeting of minds over the legitimacy of his tactics, especially bowling bouncers at youngsters. As far as Gilchrist was concerned, if David Booth was good enough to bat at number three, he should expect the treatment.

Upset by Oldham's unilateral action, Middleton lodged a strong protest to the CLL against illegal interference. It should have been the umpires' decision to stop play if Gilchrist's bowling was illegal. At an emergency meeting the following Friday, the CLL committee discussed the umpires' match report which confirmed that Gilchrist's bowling was legal and, consequently, Oldham were fined £5 and Lawton was severely censured. Yet, equally, there were those such as Werneth's president, Councillor Grenville Mills, who thought Middleton had failed to restrain Gilchrist and Rochdale's S.L. Barlow, who complained that the umpires had turned a blind eye to Gilchrist's throwing. His claims were endorsed by S.S. Fletcher of Ashton who'd tackled an umpire about Gilchrist's action and was told that he was staying out of trouble. 'Everybody in the league knows Gilchrist bowls unfairly,' Fletcher commented. He also mentioned Gilchrist's predilection for bowling occasional beamers, a ball so dangerous that it had caused West Indies to dispense with his services.

The presence of Gilchrist did not evoke tranquillity in the league any more than in Test circles, wrote Rex Pogson in more critical vein than the previous year. 'Gilchrist's bowling was the decisive factor in Middleton's success, and he headed the league averages with 145 wickets at 7.91 runs each. He was remarkably consistent and his speed baffles everyone. Nevertheless, throughout the season complaints were made that he intimidated batsmen by the frequency of his bumpers and bouncers and there were numerous incidents during games, culminating in the Oldham captain taking his batsmen off the field. The League Committee censured Oldham, and was undoubtedly right in doing so, since the umpires are in charge of the game, but one cannot help regretting that a firmer line was not taken earlier in the season. There can be no doubt that Gilchrist's whole attitude was often needlessly provocative, the pit of it being that he is a fine bowler capable of achieving results without recourse to such methods.'

Similar sentiments about Gilchrist were expressed by the *Oldham Chronicle*. 'Protest, walk-offs, bumpers and beamers; demonstrations by crowds and players alike; these do not give the Central Lancashire League a good name. Let it be sufficient to say that Gilchrist is a great bowler. He is too fast for the ordinary league amateur. He is also a different man on the field than he is off. That difference, combined with his threatening speed, is probably the root of all trouble. One thing is certain. Again, he has won the League Championship for his club Middleton. I don't rate Middleton as impressive as a team this summer, but Gilchrist was better, if anything, on the hard wickets, as his tally of 145 wickets shows.'

'That year 99 of his victims were clean bowled,' recalled team-mate Paul Rocca. 'I was the only player in the field in front of the wicket most games. Gilly always had four slips and two gullies.'

On Saturday, 5 September, in Middleton's final fixture, Gilchrist had a confrontation with Radcliffe captain Bill Moore, waving a stump in his face, before the umpire and non-striker Gary Sobers separated them. Sobers, Radcliffe's professional, who was never intimidated by Gilchrist, hit a sublime 101, his eighth century of the season, during which he treated his fellow West Indian with scant respect. The latter, though, had the last laugh, bowling him and blowing away the rest of the side, helping Middleton to a satisfying five-wicket victory. After the match he was due to travel to London for a charity game on the following day with Sobers, Collie Smith and Tom Dewdney, but when he failed to turn up at the appointed hour the others left without him. At 4.45am, as they approached a bend on the A34 near Stone in Staffordshire, they collided with a cattle truck. Sobers, who was driving, and Dewdney, in the front seat, received only minor injuries, but Smith, lying across the back seat, suffered a severe spinal injury and died in hospital three days later.

Smith's death plunged the world of cricket into shock and grief. From humble roots in Jamaica, he wasn't only a highly talented all-rounder with a glittering future, his sunny temperament and genuine goodness made him universally loved, not least at Burnley where he'd been the pro the previous two years. A service of remembrance was held for him at their Turf Moor ground before their final game in which Gilchrist guested for the club and accepted a reduced match fee so that proceeds could go towards Smith's family. Although he'd lost a close friend, who'd kept him out of a number of scrapes, he didn't let the occasion get to him, finishing with eight wickets. Later, during the next week, he collected Sobers, who was later fined £10 for careless driving, and Dewdney from hospital in Stoke and drove them back home.

With Gilchrist's departure, Middleton lined up Wes Hall as their professional for 1960 and when he had to withdraw at the last minute the club took a gamble by appointing the relatively unknown Basil D'Oliveira, a Cape coloured South African, in his place. On his arrival in Lancashire, Gilchrist was his first visitor, turning up at the home of his landlady, Mary Lord, saying, 'Can I see this fellow, Basil?'

Having introduced himself, Gilchrist invited D'Oliveira around to his home and told him everything he needed to know about the CLL, the players and the grounds. He continued to take an interest in him and chauffeured him in his car to the Sunday matches organised by Cec Pepper, for which his team – comprising the likes of Sobers, Ramadhin and Hall – could make up to £15 (worth about £300 in 2023) a game. 'I think Roy Gilchrist and Cec Pepper were the two people who did most towards helping me to settle down in those days,' D'Oliveira later remarked.

Yet gratitude aside, he found that the challenge of living up to Gilchrist's reputation brought its own tensions. He wrote, 'They still talked of him in the pubs and in the streets. "What about when old Gilly did so and so?" "Old Gilly would have knocked that lot over." He had earned his immortality. In his first year he had taken 140 [sic] wickets and hit the stumps 110 times. Nobody was going to beat that sort of achievement, yet I had to get myself in the ratings. My professional pride was at stake.'

It was to D'Oliveira's credit that he overcame an uncertain start in English conditions to flourish with Middleton and take a big step along the road that led to his England debut in 1966 and his subsequent success in Test cricket.

Chapter 6

Ungentlemanly Conduct

FEELING UNAPPRECIATED by the CLL, Gilchrist was only too happy to move to Bacup, a well-preserved mill town in the Rossendale valley some 20 miles north of Manchester, during the winter of 1959/60. Living in a small terraced house close to the cricket ground, he and his family quickly adapted to their new surroundings, winning the hearts of the local population.

Bacup Cricket Club were one of the founding members of the Lancashire League, established in 1890 and comprising 14 clubs based in mill towns and large villages in the Blackburn–Burnley area. Operating outside the auspices of MCC and with playing conditions similar to the CLL, it proved a much more egalitarian and parochial outfit than the first-class game, its self-contained communities intensifying the local rivalries on the field.

Like the CLL, Lancashire League clubs were permitted to field one professional and those gracing the league included such illustrious names as S.F. Barnes, England's greatest bowler, and Bobby Peel, one of the finest all-rounders in the game's history. Such players raised the standard of the cricket and swelled the gate, even when attendances were beginning to drop off in the

1950s, so Bacup would have seen the hiring of Gilchrist as a sound investment.

Situated on a steep hill above the town adjoining narrow streets of terraced houses, its attractive Lane Head ground had played host to a number of renowned overseas professionals, most notably the Australian fast bowler Ted McDonald in the 1930s and Everton Weekes in the 1950s.

Overcoming the alien weather conditions, so very different from his homeland in Barbados, Weekes's brilliance as a batsman was such that he still holds the highest batting average and most centuries in Lancashire League history overall. His stupendous feats as an all-rounder, accomplished with true Caribbean flair, and his engaging charm made him a revered figure in Bacup. Consequently, on his death in 2020, aged 95, the local council voted to create a permanent memorial to him in the town. His vibrant personality eradicated any iota of racial prejudice, so when Gilchrist arrived in 1960, his colour was immaterial.

He came with the reputation of a firebrand, with local cricket correspondent Alf Thornton predicting blood on the pitch. The Barbadian fast bowler John Holder, later an international umpire, recalled visiting Bacup as a teenager and being taken to a league match by his hosts. He wrote, 'There was a large crowd noisy and spirited, quite unlike the gentle ripples of applause that came from the deck-chaired supporters surrounding playing areas in Surrey. Everybody was getting excited because the Bacup fast bowler was clattering heads and wickets and it was clear even to my unsophisticated eye that he couldn't care less which; skull or stumps – it made no difference to him. In awed, hushed tones, I was informed that the black, for yes, he was indeed black, fast bowler was the Bacup pro, and e' were in t' mood that day. His name, I later discovered, was the notorious Roy Gilchrist. His name may well have been mud in the higher echelons of the game but he was a legend in Bacup.'

Keen to mend his ways after recent troubles and under a strict captain in Fred Mitchell whom he greatly respected – he was later to give him his West Indian cap – Gilchrist caused little trouble at Bacup. Former team-mates recall him as genial company, limited in conversation and with the chuckle of a little boy. Although competitive as ever, he used the bouncer sparingly and the one occasion he bowled a beamer – at Haslingden's Cliff Moore – which crashed into the sightscreen, he was admonished by Mitchell and warned off any repetition. 'Gilchrist bowled fair against us, until this one incident,' commented Haslingden's veteran opener Jack Cronkshaw. 'He is a great bowler. He does not need to intimidate anybody, because he is capable of getting wickets by legitimate means.'

On reviewing his progress that July, the cricket correspondent of the *Civil and Military Gazette* wrote, 'In this, his first season with the Lancashire League, he is making a determined effort to live down the "naughty boy" tag which he earned when in India and which set the West Indies selectors against him. Allegations of intimidating bowling against Gilchrist have been few and far between this season.'

Accepting that he'd bowled with great pace and accuracy, the correspondent concluded, 'He occasionally challenges a stubborn batsman with a bouncer, but this season he has not sent down a single beamer.' [sic].

Despite the miserable April weather, Gilchrist's presence in the Bacup side drew the largest crowd to Enfield for many years for the opening match of the season. Opening the batting for the home side was the club's professional Conrad Hunte and Edward Slinger, who was bowled by Gilchrist for 0 with a ball he never saw. Hunte survived to make 71, deriving great pleasure from getting the better of his fellow West Indian, since the two of them weren't close, despite Hunte, later a committed campaigner for the Moral Rearmament movement, having spoken up for him on the tour to India. Slinger recalls that in the return match at Bacup, Gilchrist bounced Hunte first ball. Hunte went to hook it and top-edged it for four. Normally he would have smiled but on this occasion, he simply stared at Gilchrist.

Although Gilchrist was soon among the wickets – his best figures came later in the season – Bacup, champions in 1958, started inauspiciously, losing three of their first six games. Their fortune changed, however, when they thrashed neighbours Rawtenstall – who were missing their professional Chandu Borde – by 148 runs and bowled Lowerhouse out for 28 with Gilchrist and his opening partner Jeff Pickup both taking five wickets. They won six out of their next seven games and after defeating Colne away in early July, Gilchrist confidently predicted that they would win the title. Much would depend on their two games against Nelson, whose professional was Johnny Wardle, the ex-Yorkshire and England spinner who could bowl both slow left-arm orthodox and googlies and chinamen.

Wardle's stellar first-class career had come to an abrupt end when he was sacked by Yorkshire in 1958 and had his invitation to tour Australia withdrawn by MCC for several ill-advised press articles lacerating his county captain, Ronnie Burnet. Gravitating to the Lancashire League, his bowling and hard-hitting batting became a prime asset to Nelson, but his on-field clowning concealed a more waspish side to his personality which

Gilchrist disliked. When the two sides met at Nelson, Wardle hit the first two balls of Gilchrist's 11th over for four, survived a shout for lbw on the third and was hit in the kidneys by the fourth. Dropping his bat, Wardle marched down the wicket to Gilchrist, waving an admonishing finger and giving him a piece of his mind. On the intervention of the two umpires and captain Mitchell, Wardle returned to his crease while Gilchrist extended his run-up. Bounding in, he slipped and the ball was called a wide, much to the amusement of the crowd, especially when Wardle resorted to humour by pretending to hide behind the stumps. Now fired up, Gilchrist dismissed Wardle next ball and mopped up the tail to finish with 8-45 to help his side to a two-wicket victory.

The feud continued when Bacup hosted Nelson a month later. Having upset Gilchrist by suggesting in a local newspaper that he threw, Wardle further inflamed matters by filming his action with a movie camera from the pavilion balcony. As soon as Gilchrist saw the camera pointing at him, he objected and refused to bowl. The game came to an abrupt halt while Mitchell walked off the field to confer with his opposite number, at which point Wardle put his camera away.

With Gilchrist and Wardle both taking five wickets, there was once again precious little between the two teams in a low-scoring encounter till Gilchrist's aggressive 23 paved the way for Bacup's one-wicket victory, their 17th consecutive match unbeaten.

A narrow loss to Burnley in their penultimate game kept the title on hold till the final day of the season as Bacup battled it out with Ramsbottom. Fielding first against East Lancashire at home, Gilchrist did his bit by claiming 7-25, but Bacup, chasing 95, were in some trouble before teenager Barry Wilson saw them home by three wickets to the delight of the home crowd as they celebrated another championship. Describing him as the most devastating fast bowler in the Lancashire League for years, *Wisden* wrote, 'Gilchrist was on his own at the top of the league averages with 126 victims at a cost of 10.23 runs each, and his fine efforts left his amateur colleagues with every chance to go for victory.' Comparing his record with the previous year, Pogson commented, 'Happily there were no doubts and recriminations this time. Gilchrist proved, indeed, that he has no need to resort to provocative tactics to achieve outstanding success.'

Gilchrist called the team spirit the best he'd ever known, but despite his success, his annual £1,150 contract over four years and his iconic status with the Bacup faithful, he was once again on the move. His decision wasn't entirely surprising, since earlier that season he'd approached two counties with a view to playing first-class cricket. He accepted that he would be giving up the 'comparatively easy life of a league pro' for the greater challenge of playing six days a week, but he wanted the thrill of 'playing every day of his life'. 'For cricket is all I ever have in my head; cricket is my king, my religion, my life,' he wrote in 1963. 'And even though I will always have that big, deep yearning to play again for West Indies, I would have given up that yearning to have a regular six days a week job where the uniform is white, where the weapon is a red ball – and life is the best in the world!'

To his immense chagrin he was turned down by both Leicestershire and Lancashire. The former were deterred by the three-year residence qualification then in place for overseas players, while the latter told him something similar. Their reasoning might well have been perfectly valid, but it is worth pointing out that Lancashire had rejected Learie Constantine on racial grounds and, later, Basil D'Oliveira. Word also seeped out that Gilchrist had blotted his copybook by bowling bouncers at Lancashire's esteemed captain Cyril Washbrook in Alan Wharton's benefit match.

Two days after Bacup won the league, the club announced that he'd asked to be released for personal reasons and they had agreed. 'We have accepted Gilchrist's request,' commented chairman Cyril Lord. 'We have no complaints whatever to make about Roy Gilchrist as a cricketer. But he feels he wants to move on.' It transpired he and the committee had been in disagreement over the timing of the payments of his next season's fee. Bacup's secretary Charles Pitt said there was no suggestion of Gilchrist going to another club, but a week later news broke that he'd signed for Great Chell, a small club on the outskirts of Stoke-on-Trent with lofty ambitions. Newly promoted to the senior A division of the North Staffordshire and District League, they had used the £80,000 they had raised from their weekly lottery to build a smart new clubhouse, a 750-seater stand and an electronic scoreboard. Determined to aspire to greater things, they enticed Gilchrist with an offer that matched his contract at Bacup. 'The Great Chell club was new ground for me,' he later wrote. 'I knew nothing about their standard of cricket; all I knew was that Ramadhin was playing their kind of cricket and I felt that anything "Ram" could do I could do as well.'

'It is a shame that a man of his undoubted ability should be allowed to "escape" to the Staffordshire League, where the standard of cricket is far below that of the Lancashire League,' declared the *Bacup Times* with more than a touch of northern bias. The North Staffordshire and District League was one of the strongest leagues in the country, responsible for nurturing the former Lancashire and England batsman Jack Ikin during the 1930s and future England players such as Ken Higgs, David

Steele and Bob Taylor during the 1950s. Steele's brother John, who later played for Leicestershire, and their cousin Brian Crump, who represented Northamptonshire, were also graduates.

In addition, the league attracted top professionals. S.F. Barnes played for Porthill Park in the years before the First World War; Frank Worrell played at Norton in the late 1950s, telling the *Staffordshire Sentinel* that he was surprised by the high standard of the league; and in 1961 Gilchrist's fellow professionals included Ramadhin, Peter Lashley, the West Indian batsman, Cliff Gladwin, the former Derbyshire opening bowler, and Ikin, who'd returned to Staffordshire to captain them in the Minor Counties. These stars helped draw large crowds to watch a league that set out to play high-class, entertaining cricket in a sporting manner.

Not for the first time in his career, Gilchrist's reputation went before him as news of his signing prompted an immediate reaction from Frank Vodrey, secretary of the North Staffordshire Umpires' Association. His suggestion that his association would probably meet to discuss Gilchrist at their next meeting, in particular his action, raised concern in some quarters. Tom Talbot, the influential chairman of Norton Cricket Club, expressed the hope that umpires wouldn't try and pre-judge the issue and would give Gilchrist the chance to play before the local crowds.

Forced on to the defensive by his critics, Vodrey denied that any victimisation was contemplated either by himself or any of his umpiring colleagues towards Gilchrist. He'd always welcomed outstanding Test players to the league. He assured readers of *The Sentinel* that Gilchrist would receive a fair hearing from each and every umpire, but at a time of intense discussions between MCC and the Australian Board of Control over the question of throwing, it was perfectly reasonable for his umpires to discuss the laws to get a unanimous opinion on their correct interpretation.

Commuting from his new home in Manchester, Gilchrist blended in well at Great Chell and exceeded expectation, his 109 wickets for the season at 6.72 placing him second in the league bowling averages to Ramadhin, the professional at Ashcombe Park, but, once again, success came at a cost. Having seen off Nantwich in his first match, he was accused of throwing by their captain, Geoff Bull, who he'd peppered with bouncers and the odd beamer. It was a charge taken up by the Nantwich crowd in the return match, a provocation that Gilchrist handled impeccably, nor did he overreact when he was racially abused by a spectator at Ashcombe Park after bowling flat out.

On Saturday, 13 May, in perfect weather, over 2,000 people paying £170 saw the president of the North Staffordshire League, Dennis Haynes, open Great Chell's new stand before a titanic clash between Gilchrist and his fellow West Indian Peter Lashley, the professional for Norton. While others were blown away by the former's blistering pace, the latter's dogged 80 was largely responsible for Norton's 57-run victory.

With Gilchrist soon becoming the talk of the league, another large crowd turned up at Crewe LMR to watch him perform. After Great Chell, a notoriously brittle batting side, were routed for 37, he took the home side's first five wickets, including their professional Dennis Cox, the former Surrey all-rounder, for just one run before Crewe's Ken Platt deployed the long handle to see them home by five wickets.

There was more drama when Great Chell played host to Bignall End and Jack Ikin, the former England batsman now captaining Staffordshire. According to Doug MacLeod, a Great

Chell member, the large crowd comprised a sizable number of women drawn by the presence of the handsome Ikin, a stylist in every way. 'As Ikin, debonair as ever, walked to the middle he looked the business, sleeves rolled down and hair immaculate. Was another innings on the cards? Gilly had other ideas. Ikin took guard. I was at square leg watching. The atmosphere was really palpable. With those long arms rotating like a windmill, Gilly bounded in; a hush around the ground and then uproar! Ikin bowled first ball of the match with a beauty.'

The visitors were shot out for 32, Gilchrist finishing with 9-8, much to the dismay of two women who confronted him in the pub afterwards. 'You got Mr Ikin out for a duck,' they said and when Gilchrist happily confirmed this they retorted, amid some expletives, 'We didn't come to see you bowl. We came to see Mr Ikin make a hundred.'

In the course of his success against Bignall End, Gilchrist became the first bowler in the league to reach 50 wickets that season, 38 of them clean bowled, and the next weekend he went one better, taking all ten against Silverdale. Although the home club had tried to neutralise Gilchrist's menace by watering the pitch, it proved to no avail, since he resorted to bowling off-breaks. The one consolation they derived from the game, however, was a home gate eight times greater than normal.

It was the same wherever Gilchrist went and with takings at Great Chell greatly exceeding previous years, the club was only too happy to offer their professional a new contract. 'He has done so well we decided we would sign him for another two years,' declared chairman Len Barber. 'We know he has been approached by two or three Lancashire clubs, and we wanted to keep hold of him while we could.

'He is very happy with Great Chell and he likes playing in the North Staffordshire League. He thinks the cricket here is of a very high standard.'

As ever the key to Gilchrist's success was his exceptional speed and accuracy. The former Stoke footballer Don Whiston, who played for Porthill Park, recalled Gilchrist bowling throughout their innings from one end. 'When I went in, he was coming off a short run and I dispatched the ball for four.

'The next ball was in the wicketkeeper's gloves before I completed the shot. The look from his eyes warned me not to take liberties even when he was bowling off a short run.'

One man who defied Gilchrist was Sneyd's veteran opener Jess Hall who carried his bat for 55, in what he considered to be the finest innings of his career. With his side reeling at 51/9, he farmed the strike so successfully that the 15-year-old John Steele didn't have to face Gilchrist once. By the time Steele was out for 4, they'd put on 40 for the last wicket to earn their side a draw.

With Crewe LMR in contention for the championship, their return match against Great Chell would have a vital bearing on their prospects. Admitting to feeling really scared when he first saw Gilchrist bowl, their professional Dennis Cox prepared the team for the forthcoming clash by making them play with smaller bats in the nets and facing their bowlers from 18 yards. His motivational skills had their desired effect, since his side stood up to the initial onslaught from Gilchrist, paving the way for a brilliant 76 from Cox himself and a resounding victory. Such was the resilience of their batsmen that Gilchrist became increasingly demoralised and cantankerous, lashing out at all and sundry, antics that earned him a black mark from the umpires in their match report. Malcolm Bailey, a member of Great Chell, recalled taking a visiting French student to see a 'typical' cricket match. 'Roy, fielding on the boundary and needled by some Crewe supporters, squared up to them and a fight ensued. Roy's subsequent overs were liberally scattered with his infamous "beamers"; he was warned by the umpire to no avail.

'Bang went my French friend's preconceived ideas about the gentle, decorous nature of cricket.'

Further trouble ensued in the next match when Stone hosted Great Chell before another large crowd. The game was given an added piquancy following the latter's win earlier in the season when Gilchrist had threatened Stone's opener in the pub afterwards. Batting first on a soft wicket, Great Chell ground out 151 in 65.4 overs, leaving their opponents 35 overs to reach their target. They were given a flying start with an opening stand of 87 and when the hundred came up in 72 minutes they were well ahead of the clock. It was at this stage that Gilchrist, affronted by the umpires telling him he appealed too much, resorted to delaying tactics. 'So, after a talk with my captain I decided to go slow', he later wrote – 'slow, easy and careful. If it took me up to six minutes a ball, that was just dandy!' He lengthened his run to 35 yards, took 12 minutes to bowl one over which included four no-balls, tied his shoelaces up and when his antics provoked the crowd into slow-handclapping him, he stood at his mark and joined in. According to the cricket correspondent of the *Stone Guardian*, it was a most unedifying display, not helped by the comments of some spectators.

The umpires told Gilchrist to get a move on, a request that brought a blistering response from the bowler and twice they went to Great Chell's captain Derek Morley to complain about the delay.

With the light deteriorating fast and following a five-minute stoppage for rain, Stone, in their quest for quick runs, slumped from 105/1 to 123/7. Their fortunes were revived, however, by the eighth-wicket pair of 19-year-old Peter Harvey and Port Vale footballer David Raine. Running everything, including byes to the wicketkeeper who was standing far back to Gilchrist, they drew closer to their target until seven were required from the final over and one off the last ball. For that delivery, Morley brought everyone in close and Gilchrist ran in from the sightscreen amid a storm of catcalls from the crowd and bowled a leg-side half-volley which Harvey clipped to the square-leg boundary.

Amid scenes of jubilation from the home supporters, Gilchrist turned to the umpire and said, 'You satisfied now, man?' as he snatched his jersey and walked off. (Claims that he threw the ball at the batsman can easily be discounted since the ball was hit to the boundary.) Subjected to abuse as he climbed the pavilion steps, he took particular exception to one small man who called him a black bastard. A brief scuffle ensued in which Gilchrist threw him down the steps before he was restrained by his team-mates.

The repercussions of Gilchrist's demeanour in the games against Crewe and Stone were to prove devastating. Following the umpires' reports, he was given a life ban from the North Staffordshire League for ungentlemanly conduct. This decision, taken by a six-strong League Emergency Committee acting with executive powers, was relayed to Gilchrist at his Manchester home by phone on the eve of his departure to Jamaica to try and reclaim his Test place. The decision not only shocked him, it appalled chairman Len Barber, whose immediate appeal against the ban was rejected, and captain Derek Morley, who, in a letter to *The Sentinel*, called it the most disgusting decision he'd ever known. Players before had been warned or suspended. 'It would appear, however, that in future they will all have to be banned for life by the Emergency Committee representing the North Staffordshire District Cricket League, a thing I can't believe. I suggest they should reconsider this decision or resign or get out and let the league membership make a fair decision, a warning or a nominal suspension.'

The peremptory nature of the ban concerned 'Sportsman' in *The Sentinel*. 'The effect of the decision is that the League have laid themselves open to a charge of precipitate action and less than 100 per cent fairness in their decision. The impartial observer will be shocked that such a far-reaching sentence has been passed without the player being heard and/or without being given a previous warning.'

In reply to the growing disquiet over the life ban, not least the undue influence exerted by the umpires, John Scholfield, the league secretary, who also happened to be secretary of Great Chell, remarked that the decision hadn't been taken lightly. Gilchrist's conduct was such that the committee weren't prepared to tolerate it in the North Staffordshire League. 'The decision had to be faced in the interests of the league and cricket in general and though the committee may be criticised for the severity of the sentence they felt in all conscience they had to face it now. It was felt that the decision must be notified to the player before he left the country.'

Not surprisingly the ban was supported by the North Staffordshire Umpires' Association. They revealed that earlier in the season the league committee, concerned about the growing dissent creeping into games, made it clear to clubs and players alike that they wouldn't tolerate such behaviour. Given the circumstances behind this case, there was no alternative to the ban if cricket was to be played in the right spirit and according to the laws of the game.

Later, after the league committee unanimously upheld the ban of its emergency committee, Frank Vodrey, in response to allegations that the full facts hadn't been reported, wrote to *The Sentinel* in a personal capacity.

'Gilchrist had not been in the league many hours before I was inundated with protests about his action. Some said he threw three or four balls every over, others that he threw the lot.

'The first ball he sent down at Chell against Ashcombe Park was one of the first throws I ever saw and it nearly knocked the bat out of the batsman's hands.

'Why didn't I no-ball him? The answer is that we decided to take collective action at the end of the season, but if anybody did call him, we would give him our full support.

'Only one man did and he got his answer from Gilchrist, as did the opening batsman who got the measure of him at Porthill. This sort of language cannot be tolerated at any time.'

Gilchrist's departure after only one year wasn't only a blow to Great Chell, it also deprived the league of its prime attraction. 'Gilchrist was the only bowler to take more than 100 wickets,' wrote Arthur Hodson in *The Cricketer*, 'and as this included two hat-tricks and one performance of taking all ten wickets in an innings, it can be truthfully said: here indeed was a very fine bowler.' He did return to Staffordshire in 1963 as a guest for Knypersley in a knockout quarter-final at Norton. He was able to play because the North Staffordshire and District League ban did not apply under the rules of the new North Staffordshire and South Cheshire League.

A crowd of 2,000 braved the rain to see him in action, but despite him being among the runs and wickets, his team narrowly lost to Norton, whose professional Chester Watson, Gilchrist's good friend, took four cheap wickets. This was one defeat he could accept philosophically.

Chapter 7

Retribution not Redemption

WHILE GILCHRIST was left to ponder an uncertain future back in Lancashire following his premature return from India in February 1959, his case aroused considerable reaction in the Caribbean from press and public alike. The *Barbados Advocate*'s Seymour Coppin declared that batsmen shouldn't be pampered and the occasional beamer or snorting bouncer was perfectly legitimate. He didn't condone any disobedience towards the captain but hoped that the harsh punishment meted out to Gilchrist would be sufficient to meet the crime.

Similar sentiments were expressed by cricket journalist Michael Gibbes in *The Advocate*'s sister paper, *The Nation*. Being outlawed for an entire tour was, he thought, sufficient retribution for Gilchrist's misdemeanours, and if he could give the WICBC his assurance that he'd learned to respect authority, he could see no valid reason why the ban on him should not be lifted, and the way cleared for his re-entry into Test cricket.

When Alexander arrived home from Pakistan in April 1959, he faced a batch of reporters who quizzed him about Gilchrist. He told the *Trinidad Guardian*'s sports editor, A.G. Atkins, that he'd been sent home for various reasons. He had been banned from bowling beamers 'because this ball served no other purpose than intimidating the batsman and wasn't in the spirit of the game'. By constantly doing this, he 'flouted my authority'. Discipline could not be maintained on the field and there was no other way out. Asked whether he would play with Gilchrist again, Alexander replied, 'Do you have to ask me that?' Whether or not Gilchrist represented his country again was a matter for the WICBC, although two months later he changed his position by stating publicly that he wouldn't play again with Gilchrist. The fact that the board reappointed Alexander captain for the 1959/60 series against England, in preference to Worrell, a man more sympathetic to Gilchrist and his return, gave an early hint of their thinking. After digesting both Alexander's tour report of India, and that of manager Berkeley Gaskin, the board announced in July 1959 that they fully upheld the unanimous action taken against Gilchrist. Their statement added, 'Having regard to several previous incidents in which Gilchrist was warned and given a chance of improving his behaviour, the Board, in the best interests of West Indies cricket, cannot invite Gilchrist to play in the MCC tour of the West Indies from December to March next.'

The board's hard line was bitterly condemned by Charles Chichester, the sports editor of British Guiana's *Daily Chronicle*, who argued that Alexander should be dropped, not Gilchrist, a view that was totally at variance with Errol Townshend in the Jamaican tabloid *Public Opinion*. He wrote, 'One must therefore conclude that Mr Chichester, having most of the facts at his disposal, is one of those whose only interest in the game is to win and such things as dispute, obedience to one's captain, fair play, sportsmanship and decency count for little on the cricket field.'

Chichester's contention that Gilchrist should play because it was a home series against England would be treated with the contempt it deserved for no man was indispensable.

Townshend's staunch defence of cricketing values was endorsed by fellow Jamaican Strebor Roberts, who thought there would be few regrets among the world cricketing public to Gilchrist's omission. 'The Board's courageous decision merits the support of all persons with a genuine interest in sport, all that sport stands for, and any self-respecting citizen.'

West Indians, and particularly Jamaicans, were sad that Gilchrist, who'd established himself as the world's fastest bowler, should leave the scene of his glory as rapidly as he'd entered it, added Roberts. 'But the game is bigger than the player; a fact the turbulent Gilchrist had failed to appreciate, and he now knows that no man is indispensable whether it be in sport or in any other sphere of endeavour.'

Gilchrist's conduct, not only in India but also on the England tour of 1957 and back home against Pakistan, had been poor. He really was on disciplinary trial on the Indian tour. And not only had he failed to pass the test there, 'but he made matters worse by being guilty of some of the most outrageous doings in the history of the game'.

Roberts continued, 'Yes, the "problem child" became a greater problem not only to his captain, Alexander, manager Gaskin, and the tour committee in general, but to all the other members of the touring party as well. He made life unhappy for everybody on the tour.'

The members of a touring team were more than ambassadors; they were, in a real sense, missionaries, 'and this spirit must be demonstrated not only where the host country is concerned, but also it must at all times be in evidence among the members of the touring team … This Gilchrist failed to realise.'

Although the Gilchrist case had no parallel in West Indian cricket, Roberts recalled that Lala Amarnath, who was sent home from India's tour of England in 1936, had redeemed himself to the extent that he subsequently became captain of India, and occupied a leading position in its cricketing administration. 'Very well then, if Gilchrist is capable of re-orientating his approach to the game he can come again, and no doubt regain his place in West Indian cricket. What has happened should have a most sobering effect upon him and others like-minded who think that winning is all that matters.

'After all, long after the cheering has ended what remains is the spirit in which the game was played.'

It was now that Gilchrist chose to tell his side of the story in an interview with the *Daily Mail* in London and three interviews with *The Gleaner*. He confessed that he'd been expecting a ban from the WICBC, a body he didn't respect, and revealed that there had been a serious rift between him and Alexander for some time, a rift exacerbated by their respective backgrounds.

In further articles he went on to defend his use of the bouncer, even against lower-order batsmen, as the fast bowler's only weapon and claimed that the WICBC didn't want him in the team. (So keen was he to play Test cricket again that he contemplated moving to Pakistan in December 1959 to play for Valika Textile Mills of Karachi and qualify for that country.)

Gilchrist's revelations prompted a fierce debate throughout the Caribbean. Many were appalled by his hard-nosed approach. 'I wonder how Gilchrist would take it if he was batting and after hitting the bowler for four, the next delivery hit him on the head. Can you imagine the serious things that would have happened if the Indians had a fast bowler with Gilchrist's speed and attack?' wrote Jack Horner in a letter to *The Gleaner*. Another reader wrote that Gilchrist's background had nothing to do with this matter. 'We have had great West Indian cricketers who never graced a secondary school nor came from rich surroundings; yet their behaviour on tour was exemplary.'

To *The Gleaner*'s Jack Anderson, Gilchrist's career stood on the brink of complete oblivion. No one could deny that his conduct on both of his tours and in the series against Pakistan had been unacceptable. 'There are some who would like the West Indies Cricket Board to publish what Gilchrist really did. Gilchrist himself, I am sure would not wish it.

'He has, however, done so much harm to himself in his press interview that it will take a great deal of wishing and making up on his part to be reconsidered as a good boy and cricketer worthy of his place as a sportsman and not only for the number of wickets he may be able to take, by the Board of Control which indeed has been ever tolerant.'

Anderson's view was endorsed by Seymour Coppin. 'The article that appeared under his name certainly showed no repentance, only a coarse boastfulness. He might have headed them "MY FAREWELL TO WEST INDIES CRICKET" by Roy Gilchrist for certainly nothing but a miracle now could have him reinstated in West Indian cricket.'

Others were more sympathetic. Tommy Scott wrote to *The Gleaner*, 'The game of cricket is always bigger than the man and you cannot fit a square peg in a round hole. If Gilchrist is a rough diamond, then it is our job to polish him up.'

Following some spiteful letters about Alexander, who wasn't in a position to answer back, Cecil Marley, a former captain of Jamaica

Gilchrist and his close friend Wes Hall arriving in England by boat, April 1957.

Gilchrist bowling at Eastbourne in the opening match of the West Indies' tour of England, 1957.

Gilchrist in perfect side-on position in his delivery stride.

West Indies in England 1957. John Goddard, the captain, is seated front row, third from the left.

Gilchrist, left, with joint manager Tom Peirce and Alf Valentine, right, receiving mail from home.

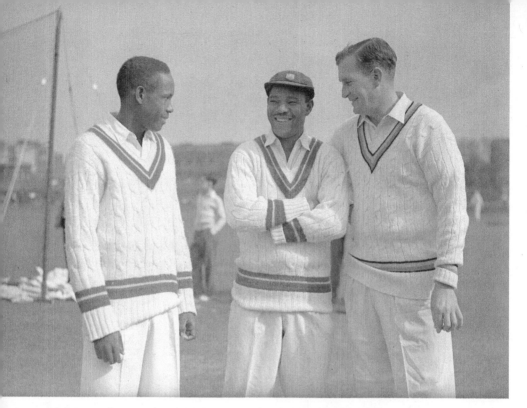

Gilchrist with
Everton Weekes
and Jim Laker
before the fourth
Test at Headingley.
Laker subsequently
accused Gilchrist of
throwing.

Gerry Alexander,
West Indies captain
from 1958-60,
who sent Gilchrist
home from India for
insubordination.

Wes Hall in full cry. He and Gilchrist proved a formidable combination in India in 1958/59.

Collie Smith, Gilchrist's fellow Jamaican and close friend, who was killed in a car accident in Staffordshire in 1959.

Frank Worrell, a father figure to Gilchrist. He later captained West Indies from 1960–63 but was unable to persuade the selectors to recall Gilchrist.

Rohan Kanhai, left, and Gary Sobers, right, brilliant batsmen and loyal team-mates of Gilchrist.

Gilchrist after a minor car accident in Stoke, 1960.

nd **Burnley News**   ESTABLISHED 1852   PRICE THREEPE

WHILE THE SIGNING IS COMPLETED . . .

THE SIGNING about to be completed. Mr Eastwood, Mr Hayes and Mr Lord look on while Roy Gilchrist puts pen to the contract.

Gilchrist signing for Lowerhouse in the Lancashire League, 1964. He only lasted one season after falling out with club chairman Bob Lord.

. . . THE FAMILY INSPECT THE GROUND WHERE HE WILL PLAY

Wanted – a crystal ball for the foreman

THREE types of shop steward were defined by a member of he Burnley Institute of Indus-

trial Supervisors, speaking to Burnley Rotary Club on Monday. There were, said Mr T. Harrison. The militant, usually Communist shop steward who was there simply to disrupt the theories of the management. The militant, non-Communist, who could bring co-operation, reason and understanding to bear, but who didn't get very far with his own members.

and one of its representatives on the WICBC, gained permission from his colleagues to tell their side of the story. In a statement issued to *The Gleaner*, he revealed that Gilchrist's high noon at Amritsar was but the culmination of a litany of transgressions that had tainted his Test career: the docking of half his tour bonus in England in 1957, his egregious behaviour at the Queen's Park Hotel, Trinidad, during the Pakistan tour, and numerous incidents of insubordination in India. He concluded, 'I have refrained from setting out here certain revolting aspects of his conduct which I consider should not be put in print. When the reports of the Captain and Manager were received, Gilchrist was written to by the Secretary of the Board and his reply was an apology. No attempt was made by him to justify his actions or excuse himself.'

In line with the WICBC's decision, the Jamaica Cricket Board also banned him from playing against MCC. It was a ban supported by Gerry Gomez, chairman of the West Indies selectors, who thought it in the best interests of their cricket, *The Gleaner* and the *Daily Telegraph*'s influential cricket correspondent, E.W. Swanton. He reckoned that no authority over the years had demanded or achieved such a high standard of sportsmanship as the WICBC. In dispensing with their fastest bowler, they had shown in the strongest possible way that the game really in their view was greater than either player or result.

In contrast, the board's uncompromising line found little support among the populace in the Caribbean, not least in the shanty towns in eastern Port-of-Spain, who threatened a boycott of the two West Indies–England Tests to be staged there. 'Gilchrist was not merely another West Indian cricketer,' wrote C.L.R. James, now editor of *The Nation*, Trinidad's pro-independence newspaper. 'He was one of the plebs and to them a hero – he was their boy. They would not judge him by ordinary standards.' On 25 September 1959, in an editorial entitled 'Gilchrist', James asked whether the WICBC had sent a representative to England that summer to have a conversation with their errant fast bowler and to give him a second chance.

He opined that the board, influenced by pontifical articles in the press preaching that the game was bigger than any individual, didn't understand Gilchrist or accept their responsibility towards him. They thought they could just excommunicate him and adopt the pharisaical attitude that we were no longer responsible for what he did. 'Gilchrist you may say knows no better. But the violations against sportsmanship and decency which have been committed by the West Indies Board of Control in relationship to West Indies captaincy in past years do not give them any moral authority to treat Gilchrist as if he were a leper.'

He might be a misguided young man but he was a very fine cricketer. 'The authorities, let us agree, were correct to send him home from India. But when the whole thing was over, and they made their statements, they should then have made every effort to get Gilchrist to see the error of his ways. This has not been done and for that the Board is completely to blame.'

Weeks later James returned to the subject having visited Jamaica and discussed Gilchrist with his former employer Bill Stewart. Stewart told him that he'd never found him any trouble, but volunteered the thought that the meteoric rise of a young man from a difficult background might have unbalanced him. He'd tried to talk to Gilchrist and get him to behave in a way which would stop the criticism, but with little success.

James subsequently wrote, 'My prevailing impression was that if Gilchrist could earn the affectionate respect of an experienced and judicious man like Mr Stewart there was something in him which the Board and its various captains and managers have failed to reach.'

He called up Gomez and suggested that the board get in touch with Worrell and ask him to talk to Gilchrist, since the latter idolised him. Aside from greatly respecting his ability as a cricketer, Gilchrist much appreciated Worrell's mentoring role in England in 1957. Committed to social inclusiveness, Worrell made it his business to reach out to the junior members of the touring party, discussing their progress, listening to their concerns and showing compassion to those who were homesick or out of form. A firm believer in paying proper wages for professional cricketers, one issue which had placed him in opposition to the WICBC, he displayed financial generosity to those such as Gilchrist whose resources were limited. He also advised him on how to bowl in local conditions, how to conduct himself on tour, not least in his relationship with the press, and helped cover up some of his foibles. During their end-of-tour festival match at Hastings, Worrell, captaining the side, told Gilchrist that in such games one didn't bowl bouncers and Gilchrist, determined to oblige, preferred to bowl half-volleys and be driven for five fours in one over by Colin Cowdrey, rather than risk disobeying his captain. Calling him '"Fatha" because Frankie was just that to the young ones, the starry-eyed ones, the ones who needed "fathering",' Gilchrist wrote that he, like so many before him, 'played his heart out for the West Indian wonder called Worrell'.

'Because here for once was a man among boys; a man who could really put spice in West Indian cricket and give you something to fight for; a thing that West Indian cricket needed, and needed real bad, believe me.'

Admiring Worrell's ability to put some steel into the spine of other batsmen he partnered, Gilchrist continued, 'When Frankie played his marathon against England on their own track, I saw boys who were as tough as leather break down and cry because they felt that, by being out, they had let their hero down.'

Worrell also acted as Gilchrist's confidant about league cricket, advising him on his move to Middleton and playing a leading role at his wedding in 1958. They lived close to each other in Lancashire, played in many charity games together and when Gilchrist wanted to buy a shirt, he would drive over to Worrell to consult him.

James stated that, under Worrell's tutelage, Gilchrist should be helped to write an apology both to the board and to Alexander. This would be published and, with Worrell to sponsor him, he could be brought back into the fold, but Gomez wasn't to be persuaded. He told James that West Indian cricketers had gained a great reputation for sportsmanship everywhere and no one should be allowed to sully it. In any case, Worrell wasn't universally popular at that time, especially in light of his controversial plans to lead a West Indies team to South Africa in 1959 at the invitation of non-white South Africans, a tour that ultimately didn't take place because of the unstable situation in that country. According to Errol Townshend, Worrell's continued support for Gilchrist despite his behaviour was irrational. 'Should he persist in his demands that the West Indies should play Gilchrist, he will slowly draw on his bank of popularity and may wake one day to discover an overdraft.'

The threat of a boycott of the Port-of-Spain Tests failed to materialise amid the excitement of MCC's arrival, but the disaffection surrounding Gilchrist's exclusion and Alexander's continued hold of the captaincy contributed to the ugly riot which scarred the second Test – convincingly won by England. Alexander's treatment of Gilchrist compounded James's conviction that West Indies should be led by a black man, which in turn embodied the broader campaign for black leadership in the Caribbean. Consequently, before the end of the second Test, he used his position as editor of *The Nation* to call for the replacement of Alexander as captain with Worrell and the reinstatement of Gilchrist.

His campaign ultimately succeeded, but his personal barbs against Alexander as captain, wicketkeeper and batsman were most undeserving. He wrote, 'I want to say clearly beforehand that the idea of Alexander captaining a side on which Frank Worrell is playing is to me quite revolting. Whatever the result of the series I shall mobilise everything I can so that Frank should captain the team to Australia.'

His strident tone appalled Alan Ross, cricket correspondent of *The Observer*, especially since James knew that Alexander was only offered the captaincy after Worrell had twice turned it down to concentrate on his studies. He wrote in *Through the Caribbean*, his account of MCC's 1959/60 tour of the West Indies, 'Who but a malicious xenophobe could write, during a Test match, "that the idea of Alexander captaining a side on which Frank Worrell is playing is to me quite revolting"? *Revolting* is the parlance of the irresponsible agitator. Worrell's great gifts as a player, his intelligence and charm, and no doubt his capacity for leadership, cannot benefit from such advocacy.'

'Gerry was one of my dearest friends,' recalled Jackie Hendriks, 'and it hurt me very greatly to hear these people going on about the colour of his skin ... after he had done such a damn good job when he got that young team in '58.

After West Indies' 1-0 defeat to England and James's campaign to remove Alexander from the captaincy, a campaign which James later conceded was unfair, Alexander willingly made way for his friend Worrell, serving with distinction as vice-captain on the historic tour to Australia in 1960/61. Given Worrell's warm relationship with Gilchrist and his confidence that he could handle him, he wanted him to be picked. 'Give me Gilly and I shall beat Australia,' he pleaded, but the board, fearing a repetition of the India tour, weren't for turning. Gomez, the manager in Australia, later said on television that Gilchrist's non-selection was due to his unruly character. He had a violent temper and 'when aroused he is quite unmanageable and I think our board would not like to stick its neck out'.

Gilchrist's continued spell in the wilderness was regretted by Seymour Coppin. He thought that his early return from India and Pakistan and his non-selection from the team to play England sufficient punishment for his conduct in India, especially as he'd apologised to the WICBC.

His omission placed a greater responsibility on Hall and Watson, since the rest of the attack posed less of a threat. A sprained thigh injury to off-spinner Lance Gibbs, which threatened his future on the tour, prompted talk of Gilchrist replacing him. Former Australian all-rounder Keith Miller, noting the lack of support for Hall in the tied Test at Brisbane, wrote, 'Let bygones be bygones, and send for Gilchrist and you will win the Test series in a canter.'

When questioned about the speculation, Gilchrist, back in Jamaica for Christmas to see his mother, declared that he would be only too happy to play for West Indies again, a prospect that won popular backing. In a letter to *The Gleaner*, the Rev. Glaister

Wright wrote, 'When the woman was taken in adultery, did not our Lord forgive her? "Go and sin no more," he said. Surely Gilchrist knows that all eyes will be upon him in Australia?

'Cannot our local Cricket Board cable the West Indies Committee to forgive Gilchrist and send him by air for the next Test? Are we always to take our Test defeats lying down or shall we snatch victory in the nick of time?'

Had Gilchrist been present in Australia, West Indies would probably have won, but, in a wonderful series, they lost 2-1. With their reputation fully restored under Worrell's chivalrous leadership, and with the majority of the public in favour of Gilchrist's rehabilitation, the WICBC lifted their ban on him at their annual meeting in March 1961. Later that autumn, prior to his life ban by the North Staffordshire League, he received a letter from Ken Wishart, the secretary of the WICBC, inviting him to play in the Test trials for the home series against India.

Urged by his wife Novlyn to accept on the ground, that the West Indian authorities wanted him back, Gilchrist then received a second letter from Wishart advising him that should he be about to sign another contract with an English league club, he should insist on a clause that allowed him to play for West Indies in England in 1963, if needed.

The Jamaica Cricket Board also invited him to play in the inter-territorial tournament in British Guiana that October and paid for his journey on the SS *Golfito*. When the ship bringing him and the other West Indian players from England docked in Bridgetown, cricket fans flocked to the harbour to catch a glimpse of him. He broke his three-week silence, telling the *Barbados Advocate*'s Tony Vanterpool, 'A glorious cricketing future still lies ahead of me. I play it hard, and that is what the clubs like most … I will forever get money out of cricket.'

He was also cheered by dock workers in Trinidad but his arrival home was dogged by controversy. Confronted with news of his life ban by the North Staffordshire League, the Jamaica Cricket Board asked Harold Gilligan, the former England player and West Indies delegate on the ICC, to conduct a thorough investigation into the circumstances leading up to the ban. 'Perhaps when all the facts come to light, Gilchrist will be presented in an entirely different light,' wrote Strebor Roberts, 'but if on the other hand, he is as guilty as the drastic action of the North Staffordshire League Committee indicates, it is time for Mr Gilchrist to be banned from any type of competitive cricket.'

His opinion was endorsed by Seymour Copping, who wrote, 'I have been accused in West Indies cricket circles of being more than lenient towards Gilchrist because I have advocated lenience in the many cases that he has abundantly transgressed.

'On this occasion, however, I am unable to ask extension on any grounds. If the Gilligan report is to the effect that he is not a team man, that his behaviour is not in keeping with what we consider proper in international circles, then let us spew him out.'

According to Vincent McCormack, president of the Jamaica Cricket Board, they would await Gilligan's report and if he was found guilty, he wouldn't play in the tournament. His opinion was contradicted by Jamaica's team manager Johnny Groves, who said that Gilchrist would play whatever the report said.

Gilligan meanwhile approached the North Staffordshire League and was given the report presented to the league committee. This he sent to the Jamaica Cricket Board together with his own report.

The WICBC also asked for the North Staffordshire League's report on Gilchrist.

On receipt of the report before their game against Barbados, the Jamaica Cricket Board wouldn't disclose its content, but issued a press release stating that having read it they decided to place it on record and take no further action. The WICBC, however, weren't so accommodating. Without asking Gilchrist for his side of the story, or taking into account Worrell's overtures on his behalf, they resolved not to consider him for the India series and when news seeped out of their decision, Gilchrist, so enthusiastic at practice beforehand, went into Jamaica's game against Barbados in low spirits. 'For the first time in my life my heart had not been in my bowling,' he later commented.

Because of Gilchrist's new-ball partnership with Lester King, Jamaica were ranked as tournament favourites. They began promisingly against Barbados by batting first and compiling a laborious 466, only for their discipline to collapse thereafter. Opening the bowling, Gilchrist had the crowd buzzing with excitement, but then, to their amazement, opener Cammie Smith struck him for five fours in his first two overs. Along with opener Conrad Hunte, he continued to flay the bowling to all parts of the ground and on reaching his fifty in 37 minutes the crowd cheered him to the echo.

Having conceded 52 runs in his first five overs in what was his first first-class match for nearly three years, Gilchrist reduced his pace the next day to concentrate on accuracy, but while he slowed the scoring rate, the openers remained very much on top. They put on 244 for the first wicket and although Gilchrist eventually trapped Smith for 127, he finished with the unflattering figures of 2-177 off 40 overs. Amidst a lamentable fielding display by Jamaica, the worst Strebor Roberts had seen from the team, Barbados piled on the agony to make 664, and completed an innings victory. 'Problem player, Roy Gilchrist, who was rated before the match as Jamaica's winner, disappointed,' wrote Roberts. 'He did not look anything near the bowler he was three years ago. He has lost his speed and action and was very fortunate not to have been called for throwing.'

Gilchrist's underwhelming performance provided the perfect excuse for the WICBC to omit him from the West Indies squad of 23, six of whom were fast bowlers, to play India. According to the *Trinidad Guardian*, his exclusion was both shocking and mysterious. While accepting that his bowling against Barbados had lacked consistency, the paper argued that he could hardly be at his best after a long lay-off.

The decision also puzzled Seymour Coppin. There had been much speculation as to why Gilchrist wasn't chosen, especially since Berkeley Gaskin, chairman of the selection committee, confirmed it wasn't due to disciplinary action. 'The truth is that Gilchrist is suspected of throwing in influential West Indian cricket quarters. If this is so, why not make a statement on why he wasn't called? His action does seem suspect to me but I am no expert – and for that matter so does Charlie Stayer's.'

As for Gilchrist, he later admitted to feeling utterly demoralised. 'I also felt sick at heart. My wife and children were a long way away, living as best they could, and I had not the money to get back to them.'

While playing against Barbados, Gilchrist received the offer of a two-month coaching job at the British Guiana East Indians, the premier Indian cricket club in the country, from captain Dr Alli-Shaw, who invited him to stay at his home. When Gilchrist told Groves of his plan to stay in British Guiana rather than accompany the Jamaican team back to Kingston, Groves told him that this wasn't possible without first obtaining the permission of the Immigration Department.

Having consulted the WICBC, who told him that it was a matter for the Jamaica Board of Control, since they'd arranged Gilchrist's visit, Groves rang president Vincent McCormack. McCormack thought Gilchrist should return to England but Gilchrist stood firm. He said he'd accepted the coaching offer and didn't see why he should be sent back to England when he planned to visit the Caribbean for two months. It needed the intervention of WICBC president John Dare, who authorised his return to England at the end of his coaching stint, to grant him his wish.

As it was, Gilchrist enjoyed his time in Georgetown, establishing an excellent rapport with the young boys he was coaching, not least because he encouraged them to play naturally. He also won the sympathy of the local population regarding his continued exclusion from the Test side. During one match in the regional tournament at Bourda, he repeatedly encountered his manager in India, Berkeley Gaskin, much to the crowd's amusement who shouted, 'There's your friend, Gilly boy,' but while acknowledging Gaskin he never felt able to speak to him.

On 8 December Gilchrist left British Guiana by ship supposedly for England. He praised the locals for their friendliness and understanding and talked about returning with his family to play there in their domestic competition. His mood was less benign when docking in Trinidad. Quizzed by local journalists about his plans, he snapped, 'That's my damned personal business.'

On arrival in Jamaica to spend Christmas with his mother, his plans changed once again, since, in response to various overtures, although not from the Jamaica board, he decided to stay and make himself available for the island game against India. Admitting to bowling badly against Barbados, he practised assiduously and played in two trial games, taking three wickets in each, on both occasions dismissing the top three in the order. In the second game, however, he was no-balled five times for throwing by Test umpire Douglas Sang Hue, a further blot on his reputation which might well have sealed his fate, especially given Gaskin's and Alexander's private conviction that he threw. Two days later he was omitted from the Jamaican squad of 15 to play India, the selectors stating that 'Gilchrist's form didn't warrant selection'. Their reasoning seemed bizarre given his past record as a proven Test player and his success in the trials. One can only assume that they had their own agenda. According to Chester Watson, the West Indies and Jamaica Boards of Control had dealt him a rank injustice, and even cricketers such as Everton Weekes and Conrad Hunte, neither a great admirer of Gilchrist, thought he'd been badly treated.

Whatever the explanation, it marked a defining moment in Gilchrist's fortunes. He left for England two days later never to play a first-class match in the Caribbean again, and his Test career all but over. He still harboured hopes of being picked for the West Indies' tour of England in 1963, but the selectors, thinking him beyond redemption, omitted him – much to his bitterness, as he informed *The People* that May.

'Lots of people who should know think Roy Gilchrist – that's me, Gilly – is the world's fastest bowler.

'Lots more people also think I should have been in the West Indies team touring England this summer. As opening fast bowler with my old friend Wes Hall. And Gilly won't say that's wrong, either.

'But I was out, man. OUT.

'That's what gets my hot blood up. That's what is making Roy Gilchrist fighting, fighting mad right now. I've had a raw deal from my own people. Coloured people. From people who've known me ever since I was an eight-stone kid from the plantation.

'Now this cold-shoulder they're handing me is nothing new. Four years ago, they tagged me as a bad boy, a rebel who wouldn't take orders.

'That was when they sent me home from the tour of India.

'And, man, are they trying to beat it out of me with a big, big stick!

'But I don't blame that sending home. I blame a little incident when I was pro for Great Chell in your North Staffs League. That, I reckon, is the real reason why I'm out in the cold.'

He concluded, 'Man, I'm just in the wrong set. It isn't enough to live and breathe cricket any more or to be the fastest bowler in the world.

'No, get yourself a fancy white evening jacket, a fancy line in small talk for the cocktail parties, and if you're black act as though you were white, only a darned sight more so.

'Then, man, you'll be a West Indian success, whatever you do out there where it counts, on the old track.'

Although he alienated many an opponent with his suspect action, fast bowler Charlie Griffith emerged from the 1963 England tour triumphant and, for the next five years, he, in partnership with Hall and Sobers, made Gilchrist surplus to requirements. It marked a bitter end to Gilchrist's all-too-brief Test career which saw him evolve from rookie paceman to the world's most feared bowler in little more than a year. Given his youth and fitness and his explosive partnership with Hall in

India, his potential for future greatness was unquestioned, but international cricket requires additional qualities and Gilchrist's reckless insubordination towards authority made him a liability in the eyes of his superiors. His dethronement was as swift as it was brutal, leaving him with only his memories as he was cast into permanent oblivion.

Chapter 8

Mentoring in India

WHILE GILCHRIST was in Jamaica during the winter of 1961/62, he received a letter from Bacup asking him to return as their professional on a one-year contract and having enjoyed his previous time there, he was more than happy to oblige.

After a disappointing year in 1961, Bacup had replaced Fred Mitchell as captain with 21-year-old Bob Bennett, who later that year made his debut for Lancashire. Bennett recalled that the first time Gilchrist met him at practice he came over and said, 'I want you to know that I won't cause you any problems,' and he didn't. The only incident occurred in a friendly against Ilkley who resented Gilchrist bowling so quickly against them.

From the start he was back among the wickets, taking 8-55 and 7-33 against Colne. In the second of these games, he upset the home crowd by hitting captain Frank Taylor on the head, a nasty blow that required a dozen stitches on his left ear. The only resistance came from opener Malcolm Blackhurst, who scored 32 out of his side's 61 before Gilchrist bowled him with a beauty that came back at him, at which point he escorted him off, applauding him all the way.

Gilchrist continued the good work in successive wins over Rawtenstall, Lowerhouse – in which he claimed the wicket of Basil Butcher – and current champions Accrington, whose professional was Wes Hall. The presence of the two fastest bowlers in the world added a touch of needle to this fixture but the conflicting approach of the two protagonists was very much in evidence. Batting first in a rain-affected match, Bacup were making heavy weather of Hall before Gilchrist appeared at number six. As a batsman, Gilchrist was a genuine tailender in the first-class game as his career average of 5.45 would confirm. In the leagues he was flattered by his position in the middle order given his lack of runs – his Lancashire League average was 9.95 – but he did have a good eye and taking advantage of Hall's refusal to bowl short at him, he hit out hard for an undefeated 32.

Bacup declared at 109/4 and with his team-mates terrified of facing Gilchrist, Hall volunteered to open himself, whistling 'Stranger on the Shore', before he was out for 10, the one man to reach double figures as Accrington were bundled out for 33 in 8.2 overs.

Bacup continued their winning streak against Enfield and Nelson, where in front of a large home crowd, Gilchrist took 8-33, including his old adversary Wardle. The one Nelson batsman to impress was Ian Greenwood, who was nearing fifty and anticipating a healthy collection for his pains when he was left undefeated on 47. After the game, while changing in a local hotel before going on holiday, his right thigh was black. 'What's that?' exclaimed his wife. 'That's Roy Gilchrist for you,' he replied. Thereafter she insisted that he wore a thigh pad.

For all his bruises, Greenwood liked Gilchrist and never felt intimidated by him.

On 23 June Bacup stood proudly top of the table, but on successive Saturdays their fortunes took a tumble from which they never recovered. Despite a maiden fifty from Gilchrist, they were beaten by Burnley by ten runs; then the following week they took on second-placed Church, whose professional Chester Watson was the league's leading bowler that year. A fearsome fast bowler with a deadly yorker, Watson had played in all five Tests against England in 1959/60, acting as an admirable foil to Wes Hall. Now ensconced with Church, he proved a model professional, his efforts on the field accompanied by his benign charm off it and after settling in Manchester he became a true friend to Gilchrist thereafter.

Batting first, Church struggled from the first over as Gilchrist, bowling with bristling pace, reduced them to 35/5. A gritty 61 from Syd Edmundson and a hard-hitting 32 from Watson improved matters before Gilchrist, bowling unchanged, polished off the tail to finish with remarkable figures of 10-75. His success in taking all ten wickets – last achieved in the Lancashire League by India's Subhash Gupte seven years earlier – won him a thunderous ovation as he led his team from the field.

Needing 151 to win, Bacup began disastrously when Watson, bowling very fast, claimed a hat-trick in his opening over. Thanks to 40 from Barry Wilson, 35 from Bob Bennett and 28 from Fred Mitchell, they clawed their way back into the game, but with Watson taking seven wickets they fell at the final hurdle, their ten-run defeat seeing them relinquish their top-of-the-table position to Church, the eventual champions.

Not only that. Bacup claimed only one victory in their last 11 matches as the batting, deprived of the services of Bennett, who was now playing for Lancashire, proved brittle and Gilchrist, so often their talisman, ran out of steam. Against Ramsbottom, he was spoken to by the umpires after questioning a decision against their professional, the West Indies batsman Seymour Nurse, who went on to score a century; then in the return game against Accrington, Hall turned the tables on him. Having absorbed every missile Gilchrist had fired at him, sparing his team-mates another battering, he bowled his side to a 30-run victory by taking 10-28. 'A shocked Gilchrist couldn't believe I would do such a thing to him,' Hall later wrote, although he accepted defeat with good grace, shaking Hall's hand as he came off the field and saying, 'Dinner's on me, mate!'

That winter Gilchrist returned to India to participate in an innovative cricketing experiment. After the punishment the West Indian quicks had inflicted on India in 1958/59, the Maharajkumar of Vizianagaram, a former president of the BCCI, tried to get Gilchrist to India in September 1959 to coach Indian batsmen in how to play fast bowling. Gilchrist expressed a willingness to go, any reservations about returning to India, the scene of his greatest humiliation, overridden by financial considerations, but, in light of his ban by the WICBC, the BCCI rejected the idea, much to the approval of *The Times of India*. Engaging a player whose participation in official cricket had been outlawed by his own controlling body would be improper, it declared, and Vizianagaram was only trying to court publicity with his 'farcical' proposals.

Following India's capitulation to West Indies on their tour there in 1961/62, the BCCI president M.A. Chidambaram contracted four West Indian fast bowlers – Gilchrist, Lester King, Chester Watson and Charlie Stayers – to India during the 1962/63 season to put into effect Vizianagaram's idea. When critics pointed out that two of the four bowlers – Gilchrist and

Stayers – had suspect actions, Chidambaram retorted, 'Even if they chuck or throw the occasional one, well, let our batsmen get used to that also.'

Gilchrist was approached by Ghulam Ahmed, manager of the Indian team in the West Indies in 1962, and he willingly signed up. On arrival in mid-October, he was asked by a journalist why there were no effective Indian fast bowlers, to which he replied, 'Man, you don't eat beef, you don't drink grog and you don't bother with women. How can you have fast bowlers, man?' It was the comment of a man, who, unlike his team-mates, made little effort to understand India's history and culture.

From his previous experience there, Gilchrist complained that many of the Indian players wouldn't talk to him 'and when they sat with you talked their own native dialects so that you did not know a thing they were saying'. Then he was involved in an incident at Kanpur. He had gone to the Post Office to buy stamps. When he asked the clerk the cost of sending a letter home, the clerk was unable to answer him, even after Gilchrist repeated the question, because he couldn't understand him.

Infuriated at the clerk's ignorance, Gilchrist rushed inside the cabin, pulled him out and manhandled him. Amid the commotion, the police were called and Gilchrist was charged with manhandling a government clerk on duty. Fortunately, the Kanpur cricket authorities and the BCCI reacted quickly and a nasty diplomatic incident was averted.

Chester Watson recalls another occasion when Gilchrist became embroiled in a fight with a member of the public at a post-match social event because he thought he'd been insulted.

In line with the policy of assigning the four players to different parts of India, Gilchrist was allotted to Hyderabad, the hottest part of the country, as he wryly remarked. He was soon in action playing for an invitation XI against an Indian side sponsored by the Associated Cement Company in the final of the Moin-ud-Dowlah Gold Cup Tournament, featuring many international players. On a lifeless pitch, wicketkeeper Farokh Engineer recalls standing up to Gilchrist, even to the new ball, and claimed a leg-side stumping off his bowling. His team-mates were most impressed but Gilchrist was furious. By standing up to him, Engineer had insulted him and he was little mollified by his explanation that it was only the slowness of the wicket that had prompted his move.

Gilchrist's coaching clinic in Madras, a city of decorum where the shopkeepers were polite and the police were respected, wasn't for the faint-hearted. According to former South Zone off-spinner Venkatraman Ramnarayan, his wards were subjected to a rigorous drill of physical training and fielding practice in addition to a liberal dose of earthy cricket wisdom delivered in an accent barely fathomable to the boys whose English was shaky in any case.

The thrill of getting some free cricket tuition against a world-class fast bowler soon dissipated, since Gilchrist often bowled at a fair pace to demonstrate some finer points. Most batsmen knew better than to play attacking shots off him, but one carefree soul called Benjamin couldn't resist the temptation. A couple of crisp drives invited the inevitable bouncer from Gilchrist, albeit off a short run-up, which Benjamin promptly dispatched with a flourish. This was a fatal mistake, wrote Ramnarayan. The next couple of bouncers, delivered off his full run-up, just missed decapitating him.

According to South Zone batsman A.G. Milkha Singh, Gilchrist thought the Indians were inferior. At coaching camps for the state side, he used to bowl with the new ball to all of them off his full run. 'While he was running in to bowl, this opening bat from our state started moving about; he started moving to the leg side. Mr Gilchrist said, "Man" in a West Indies colloquial way, by which he meant to say, "Don't move." Second ball, again he came and bowled. The batsman started moving again. This time he was a bit angry and so he threw the ball on the ground and said, "I want you to run, but between the wickets."'

Gilchrist's high expectations meant that a few bowlers dropped out midway through the course including medium-pacer Inder Mohan, who played truant for more than a week. He was watching a game at the Government Arts College on Mount Road, leaning over a low compound wall when he saw Gilchrist doing the same a few yards from him. Gilchrist caught sight of him and walked towards him to inquire about his health. Fearing the worst, Mohan started edging away but Gilchrist followed him, determined to ascertain when he would be resuming practice. Soon Mohan broke into a trot and then started sprinting with Gilchrist in hot pursuit, to the amazement of a somnolent Sunday crowd.

It wasn't his only pursuit. One player in the camp who Gilchrist befriended was a bowler with a dubious action called George Thomas. At one point he was hit in the chest by Thomas. He put his bat down and said, 'George, you bat now.' They were soon running around the stadium chasing each other.

Throughout the season Gilchrist, along with the other West Indians, played in a series of exhibition matches in aid of the National Defence Fund following a recent Chinese attack on the Indian border. Although he was criticised for taking festival matches too seriously – in one match he broke Shyam Mitra's wrist and Ramnath Kenny's elbow – he made little impact overall.

Likewise, in his two games for South Zone in the Duleep Trophy, a competition originally contested by the five zonal sides, he failed to sparkle, his fire doused by the flat wickets and the lack of support at the other end. In the semi-final against Central Zone at Bangalore, South Zone came up against the grit of Vijay Manjrekar and the class of Hanumant Singh, a future Test player. The former overcame a nasty blow to the cheek when attempting to hook Gilchrist to hit a courageous 87 and the latter survived an extremely confident lbw appeal against him to score 118. Finally, when he was out, Gilchrist ran in from fine leg to congratulate the umpire.

Fortunate to reach the final on the toss of a coin after drawing with Central Zone, South Zone's luck ran out in the final against West Zone when they were dismissed for 132 on the opening day. Riled by such a limp exhibition of batting, a fired-up Gilchrist soon forced opener S.P. Gaekwad to retire hurt with a fractured wrist and dismissed Bapu Nadkarni cheaply as West Zone closed on 91/2.

The next morning, he crossed swords with Engineer, a flamboyant batsman and one of the few Indians prepared to take on the quicks. Blessed with an eagle eye that enabled him to pick up the bouncer quickly, Engineer set the tempo by hooking Gilchrist for two sixes off the front foot, much to the crowd's excitement and the bowler's fury. 'On the third ball he just kept running straight towards me, past the umpire and right up to where I was batting,' recalled Engineer. 'He was bristling with rage and said something like, "You ugly swine, if you hit me one more time I'll run up and ram this red ball into that pretty face of yours," and he even grazed my nose with the seam of the ball. All the players and the two umpires rushed around to separate us.

I said, "Gilly, when you come out to bat you better keep a steady eye on those stumps or I will be shoving them where they will really hurt … I told him to get on with his bowling. "You've got a ball in your hand and I've got a bat in mine; you bowl as many bouncers as you like and I'll hit it anywhere I like.'"

That evening at a cocktail party for both teams and on the coach back to the hotel, Gilchrist kept snarling at him. Shortly after Engineer retired to his room there was a knock at his door and when he inquired who it was, Gilchrist replied, 'It's me, man. I want a drink with you, man.'

Engineer opened up and Gilchrist came in and put two glasses on the table with a bottle of rum, seemingly oblivious to his egregious conduct that morning. 'That was his way of saying sorry – though he never actually offered the word – he was too proud for that,' recalled Engineer.

After a glass of rum, he started showing Engineer photographs of his wife and child, a rarity because he rarely talked about his family. 'He was almost in tears and he told me how much he was missing them back home. I felt sorry for the guy. He showed that he had some human element after all and after that day I regarded him just a little differently.'

With Umrigar, Adhikari and Wadekar laying waste to a listless South Zone attack, not least Gilchrist who finished with 2-143 off 24 overs, West Zone went on to make 413/8 declared and won by an innings.

The one occasion that Gilchrist displayed real venom was playing for Hyderabad against Bengal in the quarter-final of the Ranji Trophy, the first-class championship of India. Played on a sporting wicket at Eden Gardens, Calcutta, he tried to intimidate his opponents before the match with blood-curling talk. 'There was a lot of heat over the match as Gilchrist had said he would send half the Bengal team to hospital and even while choosing the ball had tested its bounce, wondering if it was hard enough to break Pankaj Roy's head,' recalled Roy's son Pranab.

Pankaj, the former Indian opener, was as unnerved as the rest of his team, and put himself down to bat at number four. At this there was a minor revolt in the Bengal dressing room, with the youngsters chiding him for failing to set an example. To his lasting credit, Pankaj changed his mind and went out to open.

His unselfishness was well rewarded when, on a taut opening day, he held his side together against Gilchrist with a gritty century. He received valuable support from Shyam Mitra, who overcame his broken left wrist to score a courageous 98, and from debutant Chuni Goswami, who made an assured 41. Although the latter had never faced anyone as quick before, his coach Gopal Bhattacharya prepared him thoroughly by throwing him tennis balls, skin peeled off and soaked with water from nine or ten yards. 'I knew it wasn't the ideal way to prepare,' recounted Goswami, 'but it gave me confidence.'

Towards the end of the first day, Gilchrist, fielding on the boundary, reacted to the barracking of the crowd by hurling a boundary flag into the stand, which led to spectators throwing stones at him, forcing his captain, M.L. Jaisimha, to move him. He then offended umpire Shani with some unpleasant remarks following his refusal to give Mitra out lbw; later, on bowling Roy, he glared ferociously at the umpire and asked him whether he was out or not. 'He [Gilchrist] was a killer of a bowler,' recounted Mitra in 2001. 'In the present day, maybe Brett Lee or Allan Donald would be as quick, but Gilchrist was brutish and foul-mouthed. Batsmen would hate to face him.'

There was further trouble on the third evening with the match delicately poised. Trailing Bengal by 25 runs on first innings, Hyderabad, with Gilchrist taking three quick wickets, fought back by reducing their opponents to 83/5. After Ambar Roy joined his uncle Pankaj, this time batting at number six, Gilchrist proceeded to send down a plethora of bouncers and a beamer which had Pankaj running towards square leg, whereupon umpire Saxena no-balled him for dangerous bowling. He conveyed his concerns to Jaisimha, who spoke to Gilchrist.

Gilchrist was in the wars again the following morning when Bengal resumed at 103/5, showing dissent to umpire Saxena, who again no-balled him, so much so that the umpires halted play while they spoke to Jaisimha. Meanwhile, the crowd turned on Gilchrist by pelting him with stones and Gilchrist, after cutting down his run, lost his potency. He tried to stop Pankaj Roy running at the non-striker's end and when Pankaj hooked him for three successive fours, he let out his frustration by finishing the over bowling underarm. Although he later dismissed Lester King to claim his ninth wicket of the match, he was outsmarted by Pankaj, whose second hundred set up a comfortable Bengal victory.

Gilchrist's summer ended in anticlimax when playing for Andhra Pradesh Chief Minister's XI against the Indian Starlets. It proved to be his final first-class match. According to the distinguished Indian cricket writer K.N. Prabhu, the BCCI's experiment with West Indian fast bowlers had been a failure. While acknowledging their industry and enthusiasm as coaches, very little talent had been unearthed and the sluggish wickets had rendered them fairly ineffective in the Zonal tournaments and festival matches. His verdict, vigorously disputed by

Chidambaram, proved the prevailing consensus, since the experiment was never repeated.

Back with Bacup, Gilchrist, after a quiet start, struck gold, taking 32 wickets in five games as the club embarked on a 15-match run with only one defeat. Against Todmorden, seven of his eight victims were bowled, including Malcolm Jowett, whose dismissal caused much laughter. Gilchrist was followed by a small dog as he ran up to bowl and although his run was adversely affected and slower than usual, he bowled the perfect yorker and went on to endearingly thank the dog.

Against Haslingden, he was bombarded with bouncers from their Pakistani professional Ikram Elahi. He wasn't best pleased and Ikram, appreciating the error of his ways, visited the opposition dressing room at the tea interval. Going down on one knee, he said, 'By God, Gilly, I'm sorry,' to which Gilchrist retorted, 'You Indians will never be able to bowl fast because you live off rice pudding.'

In the return fixture at Haslingden, with Bacup in contention for the title, Gilchrist met his match in the umpire Tommy Carrick, the former Todmorden wicketkeeper whose vociferous appealing had upset Learie Constantine in the 1930s. Despite his diminutive stature, Carrick was unafraid to confront even the most intimidating professionals. That year had seen the introduction of the front-foot no-ball law as the marker for a legitimate delivery to prevent bowlers dragging their back foot, but Gilchrist ignored the rule and most umpires were too scared to call him, in contrast to Carrick. In Gilchrist's third over, Carrick no-balled him to which Gilchrist responded that he didn't bowl no-balls. Next delivery he deliberately over-stepped the crease and hearing Carrick's distinct high-pitched shout of 'no ball' turned with a gleeful expression, the ball still in his hand. A few balls later, Carrick no-balled a legitimate delivery and as Gilchrist reacted in fury, subtly said, 'You let go of that one, didn't you?'

Gilchrist's simmering resentment boiled over in his final over of a frustrating afternoon when Carrick no-balled him three deliveries running. Having exchanged heated words with the umpire and batsman Tony Holden, he snatched his cap and sweater, threw the cap on the ground and refused to complete the over. While he went to sit with the crowd, the impasse was finally broken when Haslingden declared.

Gilchrist's spat with the umpire continued to rankle at the close of play. As was his custom, Carrick travelled to matches from Todmorden on his motor scooter and since Gilchrist was meeting friends in Walsden they would be taking the same route home. 'When you're riding on that little scooter of yours tonight, Carrick, I'm going to get you,' he warned him. 'There weren't many cars on the road in those days,' recalled Carrick. 'As I was riding over Sharneyford, I kept looking behind me and every time I saw headlights in the distance I stopped and hid in bushes at the side of the road until they had gone past.'

In mid-season Gilchrist was informed that Bacup would not be renewing his contract on the premise that a new face was required. He had lost a bit of pace, it is true, but his 92 wickets at 12.58 still represented a respectable return. What seems to have undermined him was his tendency to shirk match practices when his contract obligated him to attend two per week, as well as the cost of employing him, but this shouldn't diminish his value to Bacup. 'He was probably the finest bowler I have seen in the Lancashire League,' recollected club chairman Alan Whittaker. 'I had to tackle him about a couple of things when I was treasurer and he was difficult to approach but he was always fine with me. He always gave his all in games, though, and was a good pro.'

On the market again, Gilchrist wanted to go to Burnley. He met their directors in their pavilion, but they decided against signing him because of his reputation. Upset by this rejection, he also fretted about how he was going to get back to Manchester. Norman McLeod, chairman of the club committee, told him to get into his car and, travelling at some speed, they overtook the Manchester bus, enabling Gilchrist to clamber aboard at the next stop.

Gilchrist was soon back at Burnley, this time at Lowerhouse, one of the less fashionable clubs in the Lancashire League, who were keen to broaden their horizons. The man responsible for this change of policy was Bob Lord, the chairman of Burnley Football Club, who'd recently joined their committee.

A brash, self-made businessman, Lord's autocratic ways and outspoken opinions alienated many, but he'd revived the fortunes of the football club and he now set out to do something similar for Lowerhouse, not that he knew much about cricket. Having failed to entice Fred Trueman to the club because he was reluctant to leave Yorkshire, Lord approached Gilchrist, knowing him to be a match-winner and personality. 'We have finished with cheap professionals,' commented club secretary Leslie Eastwood after Gilchrist signed for a league record £1,300 a year (worth £21,000 in 2023), exceeding Ray Lindwall's fee at Nelson in 1952 and Hugh Tayfield at East Lancashire in 1956. He was certainly quite a catch but the pre-season optimism soon faded as Lowerhouse, the weakest batting side in the league, lost their first six games.

Not only that, Gilchrist was some way below his best with only two five-wicket returns in his first 13 matches and was overshadowed by Burnley's Charlie Griffith, who broke the league record that year with 144 wickets at the ridiculously low average of 5.20 per victim, and propelled his club to the championship. Conscious of the threat he posed, Gilchrist warned Griffith before the clash with Burnley that if he hit any of the Lowerhouse team he would retaliate.

His words had little effect, since Griffith took six cheap wickets in both of Burnley's overwhelming victories over Lowerhouse.

On 11 July, Gilchrist returned to form with 10-41 against Ramsbottom, who included his fellow West Indian Seymour Nurse. To this day he remains the only person to take all ten wickets for Lowerhouse and one of five men in Lancashire League history to take all ten wickets twice, the others being Tom Lancaster, Archie Slater, Cec Pepper and Wes Hall. His feat won him warm words of praise from Bob Lord, who presented him with the ball, mounted and inscribed, but ominously wouldn't confirm the extension of his contract for the following season.

Two weeks later, Gilchrist took 6-22 against Accrington, seeing off Eddie Barlow, South Africa's opener, as Lowerhouse recorded their only two victories of the season, and he looked forward to renewing his battle with Johnny Wardle, now the pro at Rishton.

With Gilchrist leading the way, Lowerhouse took the early honours, reducing Rishton to 36/6, but sloppy fielding allowed them to reach 86 and when the home side batted a lack of application saw them bowled out for 71, the last four wickets falling without a run being scored. Unimpressed with their side's performance, the committee held an immediate post-match inquest at which Gilchrist was berated by Lord. Holding him responsible for the team's poor form, he accused him of shirking match practice and undermining team morale, much to Gilchrist's fury. Storming out after ten minutes, he asked vice-chairman Jack Hayes why he was being targeted, before telling the press, 'I didn't like Mr Lord's attitude. Why are they saying I ruined team spirit? Why am I being blamed for the club being at the bottom of the league? It's not my fault. No one has tried harder than me. Look at the figures. After all I have taken 57 wickets so far this season, 21 in the last three games. I got five today and putting out a title-chasing side like Rishton for 86 isn't bad.'

Half an hour later, he was still fuming as he drove off home. 'My reward is that they won't even tell me whether they want me next season or not. I will be honouring my contract till the end of the season but under no circumstances will I play for Lowerhouse after this year.'

In retrospect the potential for conflict between two such volatile characters as Lord and Gilchrist was always likely, especially if results went against them. According to long-serving Lowerhouse player Brian Higgin, then a promising young wicketkeeper-batsman, Gilchrist was great off the field, coaching the youngsters with enthusiasm, but his frustrated outbursts when catches were missed off his bowling upset his team-mates and several left the club.

For the remainder of the season, Gilchrist's form remained good – aside from a wicketless afternoon against Bacup, whose new professional Basil Butcher scored an undefeated 68. In the return match against Accrington, Gilchrist again accounted for Barlow but met resistance from a young David Lloyd, who scored his first fifty in the league. Lloyd, later of Lancashire and England, recalled how Gilchrist 'threw the kitchen sink at me and I am only a young kid. He had real menace on the field, the real baddie of league cricket' ... I found Roy off the field a really charming fellow, but on the field, he was an absolute brute.'

The following June Gilchrist played his final match in the Lancashire League as Todmorden's sub-professional. Opposing him was the Haslingden professional Clairmonte Depeiaza, the former West Indian wicketkeeper/batsman who, reinventing himself as a fast bowler, forced Todmorden opener Kevin Wilkinson to retire hurt with a nasty blow around the eye.

The accident spurred Gilchrist into action, especially since there was little love between him and Depeiaza. For half an hour, the latter weathered the storm before he fended Gilchrist to leg slip, much to the bowler's delight. It was the last of his 472 wickets in the Lancashire League at 10.76.

Chapter 9

'I don't play in friendlies,
even on Sundays'

FOR WELL over a decade Gilchrist plied his trade in the Lancashire League and CLL, continuing to show that same aggression that had marked his Test career. Craig Orr, a sports writer in Manchester with the *News Chronicle*, invited a newly arrived cricketer to bowl at him in the nets. The first ball he never saw, the second one hit him on the head and the third one struck him on the arm. The mystery cricketer was Gilchrist. On one occasion Gilchrist was practising in Whitworth Park in Manchester with two pick-up elevens and when he thought someone was batting for too long, he bowled him a bouncer.

In the leagues he left a trail of destruction whenever he played. In an age of minimal protection for batsmen, his extreme pace often inflicted pain on weekend amateurs. Bob Turner, the chairman of the Lancashire League club Enfield, used to relate the story that whenever his team batted against Wes Hall and Charlie Griffith they left bruises, but when they batted against Gilchrist, he left bloody holes. Not surprisingly, his opponents didn't always sleep easily on Fridays and more than a few arranged their summer holiday whenever he was in town so they didn't have to face him. Similarly, one promising young batsman in the CLL, down to play in a benefit match, quit playing for umpiring after learning that Gilchrist was opening the bowling for the opposition.

One novel plan of dealing with Gilchrist was devised by the captain of Royton, Donald Longbottom. Trying to keep the peace with him, he placed himself at slip and whenever Gilchrist hit the ball he would say, 'Oh good shot, Roy' or 'Well played, Gilly.' 'The Doc's idea was to mollify him,' recalled Royton team-mate John Cleary. 'Did it work? Absolutely not. The first ball I faced was so quick I didn't even see it.'

Another ploy was to deliberately goad him in the hope that he would lose his cool and start spraying it about – a ploy that only worked if the batsman was brave enough to withstand the sustained assault he would now unleash.

Conscious of his reputation as the world's fastest bowler, Gilchrist proudly played up to it, once resorting to anger when someone suggested that Hall was quicker than him. He certainly presented a terrifying sight to the batting side with his slow walk back to his mark, his explosive run to the wicket and his lightning-fast deliveries. Aside from his speed, his action made him deceptive, the batsman not seeing the ball from shoulder height, just in the air, making it difficult to pick up his line and length. Former Lancashire and England spinner Malcolm Hilton, then the professional at Burnley, talked himself down the order but had to face the music when the eighth wicket fell. He examined the pitch marks made by Gilchrist and told his partner how relieved he was to see they were not too short. 'Oh yes, they are,' replied his partner, 'those dents were made from your end, not towards it.'

Gilchrist made it his policy to test a batsman against the short ball and if he couldn't play it, he felt in control. Experienced players could normally tell when he would bowl the bouncer because of the longer run-up, the grunt and his landing chest-on, wide of the crease. Often it sailed harmlessly over the batsman, but much more dangerous was the short ball that flew or the bouncer that he threw, since it skidded at the batsman's throat, making it harder to pick up. Convinced that Test umpires couldn't detect his throw, especially if they were looking at his feet, he resorted to it when riled and even when his arm looked suspiciously bent, amateur umpires rarely felt confident enough to call him.

One umpire who did stand up to him was his old foe Tommy Carrick and when he no-balled Gilchrist in one game where he was some way behind the line, Gilchrist bowled the next ball from 25 yards, missing umpire Carrick's head by inches. Had he hit him, he could well have killed him.

Confronted with the sight of the opposition pro, Gilchrist found an additional yard of pace and made it a badge of honour to get one over on him. Although they could be summarily dismissed like everyone else, they rarely got hit because they kept their eye on the ball and played in line. Among those who scored runs off him were Chandu Borde, the professional at Rawtenstall, Australian all-rounder Peter Philpott, the professional at Ramsbottom and East Lancashire, and Stanley Jayasinghe, the professional at Colne. Jayasinghe, a hard-hitting batsman from Ceylon, now Sri Lanka, later recalled charging down the wicket and hitting Gilchrist for several fours, at which point Gilchrist threatened to pin him between his eyes.

'Umpire, this man is using wild language,' Jayasinghe complained, and after the umpire warned Gilchrist not to talk in such a way, Gilchrist said to Jayasinghe, 'Man, bigger men than you have tried to shut my trap and they didn't succeed.'

Although Gilchrist thought the Lancashire League was the best league he'd played in because of the standard of professionals, he was unimpressed by the tendency of the amateurs to duck rather than get into line. He rated Peter Sutcliffe of Lowerhouse, Harold Dawson of Todmorden and Gerard Cahill of Bacup for having the right technique, and he was so taken with the courage displayed by Royton's Steve Wildgoose in scoring 63 against him in the CLL that he put £1 in his collection.

One batsman who tried to get into line when facing him was the young Jack Simmons, then of Enfield and later of Lancashire. Brought up by his cricketing father never to be afraid of anyone and coached twice a week by Clyde Walcott, the club professional, Simmons felt confident enough to hold his own, but for most club players the best they could do was keep Gilchrist out and get to the other end.

A man of few words, Gilchrist displayed little remorse if he hit a batsman, a trait which damaged his reputation. Enfield opening batsman Edward Slinger, who tried never to show pain when hit, would stroll down the wicket and pat where the ball had pitched. Gilchrist would give him a thunderous look before walking back to the sightscreen and charging in. Those that decided to attack him, especially later on in the innings when he was tiring and more frustrated, tended to feel the lash of his tongue or be bombarded with the short stuff.

Yet for all the headlines about bumpers, Gilchrist's stock ball was bowled wide of the crease at the stumps with an inward trajectory and it accounted for the vast majority of his wickets.

In many ways he was a captain's dream because he loved bowling and possessed the necessary stamina to keep going all innings, but he didn't like being taken off, nor seeing catches dropped off him. When playing for Lowerhouse in 1964, an exceptional young gully fielder missed two really hard chances off his bowling, whereupon Gilchrist changed the field and put him on the boundary.

Another youngster, Ronnie Franklin of Crompton, dropped a catch in the slips off Gilchrist and received an earful from him. He wanted to move position but Gilchrist, believing he should learn from his error, told captain Doug Clarke to leave him there. A few balls later he spilled another chance and Gilchrist was so annoyed that he reduced Franklin to tears.

His competitiveness was enhanced by the financial inducements that rewarded success, especially collections, a Lancashire League and CLL tradition. When a batsman scored a fifty or a bowler took five wickets, a collection box or hat was passed round the crowd, which, with a good gate, could yield a player an additional £10–15. Chester Watson recalled the day when he got a bigger collection than Gilchrist, who suggested that they share it. On another occasion when Gilchrist and he were vying for the prize for the most wickets in the season, the former suggested to the latter that they should split the winnings, a suggestion to which Watson agreed, but when Gilchrist came out on top, he kept all the winnings for himself.

Gilchrist's love of cricket was such that he was always willing to play, be it for a West Indian social team or in a benefit game, but his fiercely competitive attitude wasn't appropriate for such relaxed occasions. Alan Haigh, the Nelson wicketkeeper, kept wicket to him in a charity match when he forced an opposing batsman to retire hurt with a broken toe. 'You know, Roy, this is a friendly match,' Haigh told him, to which Gilchrist replied, 'I don't play in friendlies.'

Haigh's team-mate at Nelson, Jack Schofield, recalled the Bishop of Burnley, the Rt. Rev. George Holderness, captaining the Nomads against the Police in a charity match in 1960 and coming in to face Gilchrist on a hat-trick. The expectation that he would be given one off the mark soon evaporated when Gilchrist bowled him first ball, much to his dismay as he trudged off disconsolately.

Simmons recalled playing against a West Indian XI in a benefit match and facing Gilchrist. Having hit him through the covers for four, he was warned by a fielder to 'watch it'. The next ball was a beamer and, as Simmons tried to get out of the way, the ball hit his bat and flew out of the ground. 'What do you think you're doing, Gilly?' captain Rohan Kanhai said to him. 'Have a rest.' Gilchrist apologised to Simmons afterwards and predicted that 'this young lad will be quite a good cricketer in the future'.

Another to experience Gilchrist's hard-nosed approach was Whit Stennett, who hailed from the fishing village of Dry Harbour in Jamaica, and who'd first encountered him in 1954 when they faced each other on the cricket field. In 1959, armed with a suitcase filled with cricket gear and just £50, Stennett made his way to England to better himself, the beginning of a new life working in the Post Office and in local government. In 2003, he became the first black Lord Mayor of Trafford. Bumping into Gilchrist on his second day in England at the local greengrocers in Moss Lane East, he was immediately invited to play in a benefit match that weekend against the Press Association. Warned by

Gilchrist that clubs expected the best of West Indians, whether they be amateur or professional, Stennett found himself bowling to the Lancashire cricket journalist and league cricketer John Kay, who hit him for three fours. 'Sten, he's not your sugar daddy,' Gilchrist admonished him. 'Shake him up.'

Stennett did precisely that by breaking Kay's jaw. 'Go and tell him you're sorry but you don't really mean it,' Gilchrist remarked to him as Kay was carted off to hospital.

In another friendly between a West Indian XI and the Police, Gilchrist's good friend Euton Christian was umpiring, but he didn't want to continue when Gilchrist was bowling so he persuaded their mutual friend Ed Allen to take over. Allen recalled Gilchrist bowling a swinging full toss to which the batsman got an inside edge off his thigh for four. As Allen signalled a boundary, Gilchrist disputed the decision, claiming it was four byes. 'No, I gave it four, Roy,' Allen told him. 'I'm the umpire here.'

He caused trouble at Blackpool in 1959 when Middleton played the home side in a Sunday friendly. Hanif Mohammad, their professional, invited Gilchrist, who was playing for the opposition, to a lunch of meat and kidney curry at his home. As he tucked into a generous helping, Gilchrist suddenly said, 'Man, you are my friend here but when you are in the middle, we will be enemies.' 'I was amazed at his comment,' Hanif recalled, 'because I had not invited him home to entertain him because he was a fast bowler whom I had to face in the friendly matches. I told him, "Gilly, don't be serious. I have not invited you because I have to face you in the match. It is only a friendly match anyway. Don't get so worked up."'

Chasing 110 to win, Blackpool, led by Hanif, shaped up well. His partner steered Gilchrist over the top of gully, and then asked him, 'How did you like my shot?' The next ball Gilchrist took a long run-up and bowled a scorching beamer. It was so fast that while the batsman managed to stop it only the handle of his bat remained in his hand while the blade flew away.

'The crowd started to hoot Gilchrist for his loss of temper,' Hanif wrote. 'Angered by this reaction, next ball, he took such a long run up that he reached near the sightscreen, and the spectators started calling for the gate to be opened so that he could walk right out of the ground.'

This time the batsman was bowled off a very quick yorker. The heckling continued and when he was no-balled three times by umpire Tom Austin, a former Blackpool player, he snatched his sweater and stalked off to the pavilion. Ordered back by Eric Price, the former Middleton professional, he returned slowly to complete his over, but when he finished it, he began arguing vehemently and Price had to intervene again. Eventually he bowled three more overs at half speed as Blackpool won by seven wickets.

Despite his flawed temperament on many of these occasions, Gilchrist was a prime attraction for any beneficiary because of his ability to attract the crowds. Australia's captain Richie Benaud recalled playing for John Rutherford at Grimsby, where he was guest professional, in 1960. Rutherford tried to get Gilchrist to play in the game, but following their spat the previous year, he declined. Not to be defeated, Rutherford asked the local newspaper editor to run a full-page story revealing how he, Rutherford, had seen off Gilchrist with ease, confirming his belief that he wasn't that fast, and regretting the fact that he would be denied the opportunity to show the people of Grimsby how to handle him.

The ploy worked to perfection. On receipt of a second invite, along with the enclosed article, Gilchrist sent a message saying that when he played in the game, he would separate Rutherford's head from his body. His presence and the pre-match verbal sparring guaranteed Rutherford a capacity crowd and although he had to withstand the full treatment from Gilchrist, the occasion did wonders for his bank balance.

In June 1961 Gilchrist played for the British band leader Vic Lewis in a benefit match for Crewe LMR captain Dennis Cox. Lewis wrote, 'After arriving at Crewe in time for Sunday lunch, I went out to toss with the opposing captain, Geoff Bull and I won the toss and put his team in to bat. I had Roy Gilchrist in my side, known as the fastest thing on two legs and a potential menace to his enemies on the cricket field. The game commenced at a gentle pace with Gary (Sobers) and Reg (Scarlett) bowling. At the falling of the fourth wicket, the distinctive figure of Geoff Bull emerged from the pavilion. Portly, padded, sweatered and capped, Bull strode across the field. Simultaneously, Roy Gilchrist came up to me, "Give me the ball, skipper!" I replied, "I'll tell you when I want you to bowl." Seconds later, as he approached the batting crease, Bull said to me in a low voice, "You won't be bowling Gilchrist, will you?"

'This was becoming an annoyance. "What's it got to do with you?" After Bull had scored what I considered to be enough runs, I called Roy over and said, "OK, You're on!" He told me what field he wanted set, four slips, two gullies, two leg slips, me at mid-off.

'Marking out his run, Gilly nearly left the field. He delivered something supersonic. Geoff Bull was foolish enough to take his eye off the ball, turning round in the opposite direction to duck. Gilly's ball hit him in the kidneys and knocked him out. The belligerent bowler went charging down the wicket, bent over Bull and roared, "Serves you right."'

While Sobers restrained Gilchrist, Cox told Lewis at tea that Bull had recently accused Gilchrist of throwing and this had been Gilchrist's revenge.

During Rohan Kanhai's benefit match at Blackpool in 1962, Gilchrist clashed with former Barbadian wicketkeeper-batsman Clairmonte Depeiaza. Following in the long tradition of fierce rivalry that existed between Jamaica and Barbados – the former thought the latter small-minded and parochial, while the latter considered the former illiterate and aggressive – Gilchrist used to say there were only four Barbadians he respected: Worrell, Hall, Sobers and Doug Clarke, the captain of Crompton, and certainly not Depeiaza. Depeiaza liked to goad him with classic dressing-room ribaldry, a form of humour that Gilchrist failed to appreciate, and having called him a chucker, the two of them came to blows. Fortunately, neither of them was hurt, but the resentment lingered, provoking a huge argument between Gilchrist, Reg Scarlett and Lance Gibbs on the way home, so much so that their chauffeur felt compelled to drive to the nearest police station, where Gilchrist was placed in the cells before order was restored.

Gilchrist's most notorious performance occurred in August 1963 when he played for Darwen in a friendly against a Commonwealth XI. Bowling well within himself, he sent down a good-length ball to the Australian Lou Laza, the professional for Bingley in the Bradford League, which struck him on the chest via the gloves. Before it fell to the ground, the batsman caught it and threw it to Gilchrist, who immediately appealed for a catch.

Umpire Gerald Verity rejected the appeal, whereupon Gilchrist started bowling bumpers, much to Laza's irritation. Eventually he told Gilchrist he must be mad, at which point Gilchrist strode down the pitch and punched Laza. Laza retaliated by striking him on the forehead with his bat and Gilchrist hit him with a stump.

Within seconds, the whole ground was in uproar. Other players rushed in to separate the two protagonists and Darwen's captain Ted Friend was sent tumbling in the melee. Many spectators invaded the playing area to sneak a better view, while Bill Bolton, president of Darwen Supporters' Club, strode to the middle to speak to Gilchrist and Laza.

Four balls later, Laza was out to Gilchrist and Pepper had to push the 19-year-old Ian Chappell, then the professional at Ramsbottom, down the steps and into the fray. He survived and at the end of the match the two adversaries, both sporting gashes and cuts from their skirmish, shook hands over a pint, declaring that it was all forgotten. The altercation made front-page headlines in the tabloids, but the recriminations were few. According to Ted Friend, Gilchrist was a real character more sinned against than sinning, although his conduct in these charity matches would hardly suggest this. The fact that he was a great crowd-puller meant that he continued to be invited to play and Gilchrist, being Gilchrist, couldn't resist a game of cricket.

Chapter 10

Domestic Strife

IN 1965 Gilchrist returned to the CLL as professional for Crompton, a village side outside Oldham on a fee of £20 per match, a sizable drop in income from his previous assignments. He received a friendly reception from his team-mates and the members and he reciprocated in kind. Ed Cooper, then a young second XI player, recalls chatting to him at the bar on a number of occasions and finding him quietly spoken and easy to talk to, if a bit introverted, while to opening bowler Peter Sutcliffe, he was 'a lovely man, a real winner, great to have in your side'. Before every game, he made Sutcliffe drink half a pint of beer to make him sweat – he would do the same – and while not a great tactician he gave sound advice, 'Keep trying, man, keep trying,' being a constant refrain.

On one occasion Crompton were playing Littleborough with the latter comfortably placed and needing three runs from the final over to claim the extra five overs, available to a side within 25 runs of victory or who had taken eight wickets. At one point in the over an inside edge went down to Gilchrist at fine leg who, to general consternation, let it go through his legs for four. When asked what the heck he was doing, he replied that he would bowl them out and proceeded to do so by taking six wickets in three overs.

Early reports suggested that he was something of a fading force denuded of his old pace and fire. It wasn't a view shared by Crompton wicketkeeper Brian Derbyshire. He had extra padding fitted in his gloves but still found some deliveries hard to take.

With Gilchrist picking up five wickets a game on a consistent basis, Crompton set the pace for the championship, but, following a warning for bowling beamers against Stockport, he became a marked man with league umpires. 'The general umpiring of Gilly is bad, make no mistake about that,' opener Terry Grimshaw told Roger Halstead of the *Oldham Chronicle*. 'On two or three occasions this season he has been provoked. Not only has he had many good appeals turned down but he has been no-balled when even the batsmen have admitted he was well behind the line.' Captain Bernard Halley, a member of the league committee, felt reluctant to speak out but said there were two or three umpires who liked to upset Gilchrist. Twice Gilchrist had been reported that season and at the monthly meeting of the CLL committee in August he was reprimanded and warned about his future conduct.

On 31 July Crompton travelled to bottom-of-the-table Royton for a tense local derby. All out for 121, they had the home side 38/3 when Gilchrist sent down a loose delivery which shot to the boundary, provoking some heckling from the crowd. Despite an appeal from Crompton captain Halley to cut it out 'for the sake of their own batsmen', the heckling continued while wickets fell at regular intervals till 19-year-old Mike Dunkerley stopped the rot. Displaying a calm temperament which impressed Gilchrist, he took his team to the brink of victory before his dismissal helped Crompton to win by three runs to maintain their lead in the table.

The following week the Crompton batting again underperformed against Radcliffe at home. During their innings of 106, one of their batsmen, Brian Marsh, was given out obstructing the field when Radcliffe captain and wicketkeeper Derek Bickley couldn't reach a catch because Marsh stood in his way, a contentious decision that heightened the tension.

When it was Radcliffe's turn to bat, Gilchrist's fury with Bickley knew no bounds. His first ball to him was a beamer. In his second over, his first ball was another beamer followed by a screaming bouncer and Bickley, pointing to his chin, shouted, 'Here.'

Affronted by Bickley's bravado, Gilchrist charged in, crossed the popping crease and hurled the ball at him from halfway down the wicket as the batsman retreated towards square leg. It just missed him.

Admitting that he'd never felt so scared in all his life, Bickley summoned his opening partner Bill McDonald and together they left the field. With the full support of his team, he conceded the match, much to the anger of the 500 crowd who milled around the pavilion. 'The first ball slipped out of my hand and never went near Bickley's head,' commented Gilchrist. 'He made me very angry with his attitude and his remarks. When I sent down that last ball, I admit I was feeling mad.'

Afterwards, Bickley alleged that Crompton captain Halley had encouraged Gilchrist in his aggression rather than restrained him. 'I was not prepared to bat against that sort of bowling. Neither was I prepared to allow my team to face Gilchrist. I couldn't play on the same field with Gilchrist again.'

Radcliffe official Jack Lowe admitted that there were faults on both sides, while Crompton thought that Radcliffe should have left the matter in the hands of the umpires and one of them, Bill Dixon, said Bickley provoked Gilchrist by pointing to his chin and making insulting remarks.

Although Crompton were awarded maximum points, the CLL took a dim view of the abandonment and both Gilchrist and Bickley were suspended for three matches, a ban which angered Crompton, especially since they were denied a deputy professional. (The chairman of the CLL committee, John Cortley, also happened to be chairman of Stockport, Crompton's closest rivals for the championship.) According to Crompton president Albert Briggs, such a sanction would never have been applied if one of the leading clubs were involved. Whatever the view, Gilchrist's absence badly penalised Crompton and instead of winning the league outright, they were forced to share it with Stockport.

Disciplinary problems continued to dog him the following year. In Crompton's match against Werneth, umpire Dave Tolhurst twice asked captain Doug Clarke to have a word with Gilchrist after he objected to being no-balled and the rejection of a caught-behind decision. Gilchrist showed the umpire the mark of his boot, while the umpire took exception to Gilchrist's remarks and threatened to abandon the match.

With Gilchrist in prime form, it came as a real shock when Crompton announced that they wouldn't be renewing his contract for 1967. The reason was purely financial, explained club secretary John Abbot, and had no bearing on Gilchrist's performances or his relationship within the league.

That year the committee had increased his match fee by £5 and guaranteed him a £50 benefit, a clause which didn't appear in the original one-year contract, all of which was added expenditure for a club that was repaying £12,000 with interest for major improvements to their pavilion. That said, Gilchrist was virtually carrying the side on his shoulders and the players badly wanted him to stay. Were Crompton members being asked to pay for better facilities by sacrificing what took place on the field, wondered the *Oldham Chronicle*? It was difficult to believe that many of them would prefer better social amenities if it resulted in an inferior club professional. The previous year had seen the club competing for honours for the first time in more than a decade and now, a year on, they were once again in contention for the title.

Such arguments failed to wash with the committee, since, in response to the players' request that they do whatever it took to keep Gilchrist, they said he would have to reapply if he wanted the job. 'This is a major blunder by the committee,' opined *The Chronicle*. 'A man has his pride. And with figures like Gilchrist's, it is expecting too much to ask for a written application after a two-year stay. Further, accepting that finance is the prime reason for Crompton's decision, it is difficult to appreciate the wisdom of making that decision without as much as a word with the players.'

Gilchrist's impending departure in no way diminished his appetite for wickets as he continued to run through most opponents. His 7-23 against Royton included his 100th wicket of the season and at the end of a year in which Crompton finished as runners-up to Stockport, he'd taken his tally to 126, making him the league's leading wicket-taker.

Following his departure from Crompton, Gilchrist applied to Ashton in the CLL and to Eppleton in the Senior Durham League, but with the former uninterested and the latter unable to agree terms, he ended up at Heaton in the Bolton League, a club which comprised a number of Bolton Wanderers footballers, including Francis Lee, later of Manchester City and England. According to Heaton's Chris Debenham, who later played for Lancashire second XI, Gilchrist took his coaching responsibilities very seriously. 'He used to say that a fast bowler's job was to intimidate and that he tried to stretch you to the limit without breaking you.

'Bowling off four or five paces in the nets, he would hit the back of the netting before you'd picked your bat up.

'As a bowler he always tried a batsman out against the short ball and if he couldn't play it, he'd say, "I win every time."

'His great achievement was to get me to play the short ball. "Don't be afraid," he would say. "Get into line and be prepared to be hit."'

With many players working on Saturday morning, matches in the Bolton League didn't start till 2.30pm and consisted of 35 eight-ball overs. Beginning with 7-38 against Farnworth, league runners-up the previous year, Gilchrist made an immediate impression. Their opener Peter Boardman had never seen anyone so quick. Once when he snicked him over the slips, Gilchrist walked down the wicket to five yards away and said, hands on hips, 'I'm going to hurt you so you'll never work again.' Yet, in common with many other players, Boardman found that off the field Gilchrist was happy-go-lucky and, unlike many professionals, paid for a round of drinks and was fun.

With Gilchrist leading the way, Heaton began with four consecutive wins and by the end of May were leading the table. Thereafter their form slumped alarmingly as an over-bowled Gilchrist faltered in the closing overs and the batting didn't measure up on the bowler-friendly wickets. Selected for the Bolton League XI away to the Birmingham League XI, he endured a miserable afternoon as he was hit to all parts by the lower order and had an altercation with the umpire. As a chastened Gilchrist boarded the coach afterwards, several of his team-mates wound him up by asking whether he was giving the umpire a lift. 'If I do, I shall eat him,' was his defiant reply.

Despite Gilchrist's tally of 79 wickets at 11.38, Heaton finished second bottom of the league. Hoping for better fortune in 1968, Gilchrist began the season in devastating form, displaying all his habitual aggression. Alan Lansdale, the Little Lever opening batsman, used to take a couple of steps down the wicket to force the quick bowlers to change their length and scored a lot of runs that way. An accomplished hooker and puller, he enjoyed the challenge of taking on Gilchrist and played him with such conviction that on one occasion Gilchrist ran past the wicket and threw the ball at Lansdale, shouting, 'I shall kill him.'

For all Gilchrist's efforts, they were once again in vain, since Heaton failed to win in the league until mid-June. He then endured a lean patch before returning to his best with 10-37 against second-placed Westhoughton to give his side a shock win.

He also had his moments with the bat, hitting 36 in one eight-ball over off Tonge's professional Jack Dyson, the former Manchester City footballer and Lancashire all-rounder, his 48 the one act of defiance in another dismal Heaton batting display. With runs at a premium all year, it isn't surprising that they finished bottom of the league.

In contrast to his strident approach on the field, Gilchrist presented a more emollient side off it. Witty and genial, he would happily converse with both team-mates and opponents about cricket in the bar afterwards. He had a photographic memory of all the matches he'd played in, the wickets he'd taken, the decisions not given and the catches missed off his bowling. Those who had annoyed him were rarely forgiven but those who defied him with courage and skill earned his respect.

Away from cricket, much of his socialising took place within the local West Indian community, especially in Moss Side, a deprived inner-city suburb of Manchester, where many Jamaican immigrants lived because of the cheap accommodation. There at the West Indian Sports and Social Club, or at the homes of his friends, he was happy to chat with anyone over a glass of rum, as well as eating Jamaican food, playing poker and having the odd bet. Later he also frequented the Anglo-West Indian Social Club in Oldham and drove the red van to Sunday friendlies with other West Indian teams. On one occasion, playing the Bristol West Indians, his team-mates became very drunk, thinking that the match would be cancelled because of bad weather, but Gilchrist saved their blushes by bowling the opposition out cheaply.

Although not a great aficionado of music, he linked up with an all-Jamaican soul band, which included Carl Ince, recently the national squash coach of Guyana. Ince recalls Gilchrist driving them all over the country and being ready to defend them at any time.

Occasionally Gilchrist and his friends would suffer from racial discrimination. Cec Wright remembers going to a pub with Gilchrist, and some other West Indians, including Sobers, after playing Radcliffe and the doorman saying, 'You are OK, Mr Sobers, but those boys can't come in.'

'You know what,' replied an irritated Sobers. 'We are going elsewhere boys.'

Although Gilchrist was naturally conscious of his colour and suffered from abuse on occasions, it wasn't something that greatly exercised him. Through the example of Learie Constantine at Nelson, Everton Weekes at Bacup and Frank Worrell at Radcliffe, Lancashire had adopted many West Indian cricketers as one of their own and Gilchrist, while a much more divisive figure, had many friends among the local community. 'For myself, I realise that a lot of white people I know would help me far quicker than some of my own countrymen,' he wrote in *Hit Me for Six*. 'I have learnt that all right.'

In his early years in England, his lucrative contracts allowed him to splash out on fast cars, smart clothes and drinks for all, but by 1960 with an expanding family he was struggling to live within his means. (When still at Middleton he wanted to send some of his earnings back to Jamaica. He asked for £50 but was furious when given a cheque. 'I want money,' he ranted, so they gave him cash from the bar.)

A notorious driver, who took liberties with the Highway Code, he had his brushes with the law. Vince Lindo, a fellow Jamaican and popular stalwart of the North Staffordshire League, recalls Gilchrist chauffeuring him to Colwyn Bay to play in their cricket festival when he was caught by a policeman driving down a one-way street. Upset by this misadventure, he stormed out of the car and said to the policeman, 'You can't stop me. I'm Roy Gilchrist, the world's fastest bowler and I'm playing cricket in your town.'

The policeman merely asked him for his autograph.

In 1959, in two separate incidents, Gilchrist was fined £4 for speeding and £20 for careless driving and had his licence suspended for six months. The next year he was involved in an accident with a lorry near Stoke, close to the spot where Collie Smith was killed, resulting in a cut over his left eye and bruises, but was able to go home after treatment.

These accidents had consequences. In September 1962 Gilchrist was forced to appear before the Manchester Official Receiver (a person who manages the protection of assets of creditors after someone has become bankrupt) after a man to whom he owed £63 in removal expenses to his present home had submitted a creditor's petition. Asked by the Receiver if he'd been extravagant, Gilchrist replied that he had a lot of expenses. He agreed that a lot of his liabilities of £2,342 were for car hire purchases. He'd found it difficult to get insurance on his car because his driving licence had been suspended previously. After an accident in his car when he wasn't insured, he became liable for £700 to a finance firm.

With his income from cricket much reduced once he left Lowerhouse in 1964, he relied on income from regular employment and although he worked hard in his various factory jobs, mainly as a labourer or lorry driver, he invariably fell out with his employers. On one occasion when the foreman refused to give him time off to play cricket, he walked out, never to return.

Aside from financial worries, his friends detected a growing bitterness following his exile from West Indies cricket. 'Gerry [Alexander] spoilt my career,' he used to say. 'When he told you that, you could see the emotion in him,' recalled fellow Jamaican Ed Allen. 'He never got over that. He would tell you this again and again.' Whit Stennett told Gilchrist to get over his obsession with Alexander and emulate the example of Roy Marshall, the West Indian batsman, who put aside his differences with his team-mates by relocating to England and enjoying a long, successful career with Hampshire, but it was advice he failed to follow. On top of this he lacked the self-discipline to curb a certain impetuosity in his personality. According to Lindo, he never seemed to learn and if you advised him, he just got louder and louder.

'Roy was a pleasant man, but you had to understand him,' concurred Allen. If challenged, his voice would go rough. He had to be top dog and win the argument.'

When in the company of mentors such as Frank Worrell, Chester Watson or Reg Scarlett, the former Jamaican off-spinner and professional at Ashton, he could usually be restrained with a comment of 'Let's go', but not with those who liked to goad him. Whit Stennett once heard an elderly West Indian woman saying at a charity match that 'Gilly is like a pig. It doesn't matter if he is cleaned and perfumed. He will go back to the mud.'

His insensitive treatment of his wife bore a certain resemblance to fellow Jamaican and West Indian fast bowler Leslie Hylton, who was hanged in 1955 for murdering his wife. Raised in the male-dominated culture of the Jamaican working class, in which male promiscuity was common and a woman's place was in the home, Gilchrist applied similar standards to his own marriage. Not only was Novlyn, his social and intellectual superior, expected to cook, clean and raise the family, she was also expected to accept his late-night socialising, his liaisons with other women and his gambling.

Gracious and unassuming, she conformed to his expectations; keeping a bright and tidy home in Churchill Street, Ardwick, and proving a devoted mother to their four boys, Michael, Mark, Andrew and Paul.

Rarely seen at the cricket – none of the boys really took to the game – and overwhelmed by her husband's cricket talk, she preferred a quiet night out with her female friends, but while prepared to tolerate a semi-detached marriage, she drew the line at the mounting debts and persistent philandering. Confronted with the excesses of his lifestyle, Gilchrist's macho personality objected to this kind of criticism from a woman and the altercations became increasingly heated.

On the night of 2 June 1967, Novlyn was doing the ironing when her husband arrived home late and asked her to accompany him to a party the following night. She refused. When he suggested it must be because she was going out with someone else, she assured him she wasn't. She didn't want to go with him because of his behaviour at parties. He'd promised her that he would change his habits, but he never did.

'So it is all finished?' Gilchrist asked her.

She said, 'As far as I am concerned it is finished because promises are made and never kept.'

Gilchrist is then alleged to have replied, 'Well, if that's the way I will kill you and the kids, and kill myself. The police don't matter because they are not hanging people anymore.'

At this point he grabbed the iron with his right hand and put his left hand on her throat. He then pushed her against the wall and after a struggle branded her face with the iron.

Becoming frightened, he then fetched some butter to put on her face. During the night he went back to the house several times, saying he was sorry and begging her not to call the police.

The next day Novlyn went to her doctor who examined her and found a four-inch-diameter burn on her left cheek. He thought it could leave a permanent scar.

Advised by a solicitor, she went to the police and they in turn arrested Gilchrist at Heaton Cricket Club four days later. 'I suppose I shall go down for this, will I?' he said to them.

Charged with wounding his wife with intent, Gilchrist was remanded on bail until 28 June.

On that date, Novlyn told Manchester magistrates that she had forgiven her husband, while John McGuinness, defending, said it was clear that Gilchrist had acted spontaneously.

'This man was not entirely in control of his faculties at the time.

'This is not a case of cold-blooded intent to do something. Immediately afterwards he was full of remorse. Had it been done with intent to maim, disfigure or disable, he would not have endeavoured to cure the damage he had done.'

Committed for trial at Manchester Crown Court on 4 July, Gilchrist pleaded not guilty and reserved his defence, but three weeks later he changed his plea and admitted inflicting grievous bodily harm on his wife. Repeating her previous plea for clemency, Novlyn told the judge that she wasn't frightened of her husband now and wanted to continue living with him. 'He is a good father and the boys need him more than me.'

Her words had their desired effect. Despite the shocking nature of the crime, Judge Edward Steel, dispensing leniency, placed Gilchrist on probation for three years. He told him, 'You are very fortunate in having a wife who is a good woman. Very much better than you deserve.

'I would have sent you to prison for a very long time. The only thing that has saved you is the love and compassion of your wife.'

He added, 'I don't know how this will affect your career as a professional cricketer. I don't know whether people will want to play with you.

'I hate to think that English sport has descended so far that brutes are tolerated because they are good at games.'

Fortunate with his reprieve, Gilchrist told reporters that he didn't think his cricket club was interested in his private life, but his mercurial nature landed him in further trouble the following year.

On 26 May 1968 Gilchrist was watching a game of cricket at Manchester Corporation transport department's sports ground when a frivolous argument developed between one of his friends, a West Indian, and Philip Edgar Day, a white man. Thinking that Day was being racist, Gilchrist intervened, at which point a fight developed and he pulled a small knife on Neil Jones, who'd jumped on his back to take the knife off him, causing superficial injuries to Jones's face.

Losing the knife in the struggle and feeling threatened, Gilchrist went to his car and returned with a larger knife with which he attacked Jones. (The reasons for his access to these knives was a matter of some speculation among his friends.) When others tried to restrain him, he lashed out at everyone in all directions, causing injuries to three others.

At Manchester Crown Court on 11 September, Gilchrist pleaded not guilty to all four charges of assault, claiming that he only used the knife to scare people away, but while the magistrate dismissed some of the prosecution's case as unreliable, he convicted Gilchrist on two of the four charges. He was fined £15 each and ordered to pay £22 4s costs. Later, on 7 November that year, he was sent to prison for 18 months for a breach of his three-year probation order. Colin Evans, then a general news reporter with the *Manchester Evening News*, bumped into him after the case and asked him for a comment. With hunched shoulders, Gilchrist suddenly got taller as he stood on tip-toes. 'Get out of my way, man,' he said, as Evans jumped to one side. It was to be his last encounter with the outside world for the next year.

Chapter 11

'You're some old bloke who can't bowl'

IT WAS while he was in prison that Gilchrist was approached by East Bierley, a small club in the Bradford League fighting off relegation. The Bradford League, founded in 1903 and consisting of 12 clubs in two divisions, had fostered generations of Yorkshire cricketers, including luminaries such as Len Hutton, Brian Close and Ray Illingworth, instilling in them a rigorous discipline and commitment. Although more parochial than the Lancashire League, it had also attracted famous outsiders such as Jack Hobbs, who played for Idle during the First World War, Learie Constantine, who played for Windhill during the Second World War, and West Indian medium-pacer Edwin St Hill, who played for East Bierley in the 1930s.

Knowing that Gilchrist was about to be released from Strangeways prison, captain Brian Lymbery met him in December 1969 and having laid down some ground rules, Gilchrist signed for them. According to Anthony Woodhouse in *The Cricketer*, 'Gilchrist has invariably been a success in his League career, and it will be a great fillip to this village side, one of the League's weaker brethren, if he can repeat some of his Lancashire triumphs. His introduction to the Bradford League has staggered many people, particularly as he did not play any cricket in 1969, but he should certainly pep up attendances.'

Somewhat rusty after his year away from cricket and on his best behaviour, Gilchrist struggled to impose himself at first, so much so that Lymbery told him to put some devil into his bowling. Gradually his performances began to improve, not least his 6-68 which helped East Bierley to a three-wicket victory against that year's champions Undercliffe, and 8-45 against Farsley, but bowling on good batting tracks and small grounds, where many a top-edge went for four, didn't help his figures. At the end of the season, his return was 61 wickets at 19.92, the most expensive return in the league among the professionals.

In his second year he resorted more to type, reacting aggressively to dropped catches or decisions not given in his favour, and throwing the odd ball when riled, although he was never called. Despite being in his mid-30s, he could still be very quick and wicketkeeper Lymbery sustained several broken fingers on his left hand when stopping some wild leg-side deliveries. Against Farsley's Bryan Rudkin, Gilchrist kept appealing for lbws to no effect. 'If you learn to bowl straight, you might get lbws,' Rudkin told him, a comment which prompted Gilchrist to respond with two fearsome deliveries, the first of which hit Rudkin on the shoulder and the second on the head. As the ball crashed into the sightscreen, Gilchrist glanced down the wicket and remarked, 'I'm getting it straight now, son.' 'At that point it was the end of the over,' recalled Lymbery. 'I took Roy off since we could have had a very unpleasant incident,' although to be fair to Rudkin he didn't complain.

Another player to antagonise Gilchrist was Hartshead Moor's Leonard Squire, who frustrated him with his solid defence. 'Then one ball beat me completely,' he recounted. 'Everyone could hear a definite click and though Gilchrist appealed, jumping up and down, the umpire was unmoved. "Not out" was the decision. Well Gilchrist stomped around fuming. I was eventually out but at the interval he came over to me glaring. "You were out, man – you hit the ball," he said. I just smiled. "I didn't touch it, you know," I said to him. The fact is that ball actually snicked my wicket, but it didn't move the bails. I think he was lost for words at this point and just walked away.'

One of three West Indians in the team, Gilchrist was idolised by Murphy Walwyn, a 14-year-old from St Kitts and Nevis, who arrived at East Bierley in 1970. Not only did he give him his first cricket kit, he turned him into a fast bowler who went on to enjoy a stellar career in the Bradford League and was a leading light in East Bierley's winning streak during the 1990s.

Yet in his second year Gilchrist's demeanour gave cause for concern, not least his rudeness towards waiters at post-match suppers. He would sometimes turn up to a game with two or three different women and then not return home, so that Lymbery would often be rung up by Novlyn the following Monday asking whether Roy was still with him and had he been paid yet. Lymbery replied that he hadn't seen him since Saturday and that he was paid after every match. Given Gilchrist's attitude, it isn't surprising that they separated with little contact thereafter between him and his family.

At the end of 1971, a season in which East Bierley were relegated, the club decided that they could no longer afford Gilchrist, leaving him at a loose end. A chance encounter determined the next stage of his cricketing odyssey. Driving a construction wagon at Bolton Hospital, he nearly collided with pedestrian Frank Taylor, his former Crompton team-mate. On greeting Gilchrist, Taylor informed him that Crompton had yet to appoint a professional for the coming season and when Gilchrist expressed an interest, Taylor spoke to the committee, who duly signed him.

Since Gilchrist's previous incarnation at Crompton, the club had fallen on hard times with a declining membership, smaller donations from local businessmen and the departure of several players to other clubs. Looking to restore their sagging fortunes, Gilchrist, while bowling more within himself than in his pomp, still continued to take wickets at will. Against Heywood, on a difficult wicket, he was close to unplayable, but his 8-44 counted for little as Crompton in turn were dismissed for 29.

With their fragile batting line-up, the club didn't record their first win until mid-June and although Gilchrist continued to provide good value with 85 wickets at 10.75, they finished bottom of the league for the second year running.

The next year was little better. Gilchrist remained a force with the new ball but lost some of his menace as the innings progressed. Against Radcliffe, his old adversary Cec Abrahams, the Cape-coloured South African, hit him for 18 in one over to steer his side to victory and with Crompton still struggling, he began to cast his gaze elsewhere. In July he announced that he was leaving at the end of the season, admitting that he hadn't been happy with the club for some time. He bowed out with five wickets against Stockport in what proved to be his final appearance in the CLL.

In the weeks leading up to the new season, Gilchrist wasn't yet attached to a club, but, once again, fate intervened. Thornham, a picturesque village club which had entered the Lancashire and Cheshire League the previous year, suddenly found themselves without a professional owing to the last-minute resignation of Wilson Hartley, who rejoined Rochdale. Although Gilchrist was available, the committee, concerned about his chequered past, were reluctant to appoint him, but the players thought otherwise and they requested a meeting with the committee to review the decision. At the last meeting before the opening of the season, the committee recorded their change of heart with more than a touch of reluctance, 'That Mr Roy Gilchrist be appointed to fill the position of Club Professional for 1974 on a match-to-match basis, subject to good behaviour on the club premises and the premises of other clubs in the L&CL. His fee wouldn't exceed £138.'

With a return of 78 wickets, a tally that remained a record for a Thornham professional in the Lancashire and Cheshire League, the appointment of Gilchrist proved a success. In July he drew the biggest crowd of the year to Norden, but it was his batting rather than his bowling that caught the eye. Coming it at number ten in a lost cause, he hit out aggressively, taking 28 off one over.

Content with his positive attitude that summer, the committee offered Gilchrist similar terms for 1975, but the honeymoon didn't last because they disciplined him and revoked his contract for failing to turn up when selected to represent the league side. Before that, he had begun the season in blistering form, cutting a swathe through his opponents, aside from Denton West tailender Alan Jones, who hit him for two sixes and two fours, much to his irritation. By the beginning of June, Thornham led the table but thereafter their winning streak ended abruptly as Gilchrist's magnetism began to fade. In July he came off second best against Norden's John Holder, the former Hampshire fast bowler, who scored 190 not out. Recounting the game in his autobiography, Holder wrote, 'Roy Gilchrist was playing. I hit him for two fours on the trot. Not unexpectedly, he then gave me a bouncer and I hooked it for six … Anyway, after that, his captain took him off. We were 28/2, he was their pro and he was removed from the attack. He was not best pleased I can tell you. In fact, he was so angry that he took himself off into the deep and whenever the ball came anywhere near him, he ambled in and kicked it back to the wicketkeeper with his boot. At the tea interval, he was still furious and sat as far away from his captain as he could.'

Another to get the better of Gilchrist was Hyde's Alan Berry. 'Roy Gilchrist had a reputation of being nasty,' he later recalled. 'I just kept hitting him over the rope at Hyde, he ended up throwing the ball at me!'

On Saturday, 26 July that year Gilchrist should have been playing cricket. Instead, he was locked in a police cell in Manchester for a three-year-old drink-driving offence that dated back to April 1972. A warrant was issued for his arrest that December but wasn't served and nothing more was heard of the matter till Gilchrist went to the police pound to collect his stolen car, minus £200 worth of cricket gear that had been stolen, whereupon he was arrested and incarcerated for two days.

The police treatment of Gilchrist left the magistrate John Bamber distinctly unimpressed. He called their behaviour extraordinarily heavy-handed and their delay in bringing the case as something of an injustice. 'What is before me is three years and three months old, which may not in law be a special reason why he should not be disqualified. But, in all justice and in a moral sense it is, and I propose to accept it as one.' Instead, he fined him £5 and endorsed his licence.

In 1976 Gilchrist returned to the Bolton League to play for Astley Bridge, teaming up with his old friend Cec Wright, but although they made a formidable opening attack, the club still finished bottom of the table.

That summer, the West Indies were touring England and Gilchrist, as was his wont, watched them whenever he could. During the third Test at Old Trafford, he arrived at the Grand Hotel, the venue of the West Indian team in Manchester, at the end of the first day's play and sat with a few of the players at the bar when opening bowler Michael Holding walked in. Gilchrist asked who he was, and when told it was Holding, he called him over.

'So you are Michael Holding?' said Gilchrist.

'Yes, Gilly,' replied Holding.

'Well,' said Gilchrist, 'I hear they say that you are as fast as I was.'

Before Holding, a smile on his face, could attempt to answer, Gilchrist continued, 'Well, we will see tomorrow, for them couldn't stand up to me.'

The next day, England were routed for 71 with Holding taking 5-17.

In 1977 Gilchrist replaced Mel Whittle as professional at Greenfield, a village club in the Saddleworth and District League, a lower standard than the CLL. He was paid £16 a game, a sum they weren't prepared to pay Whittle. Mixing in effortlessly with this friendly communal club, former team-mates such as John Brocklehurst recall him as a great character who used to regale them with many tales of his past exploits. Cricketers he didn't rate were dismissed as Bag Carriers. He came to particularly enjoy the teas at Greenfield and the ladies made him a special meat pie every home match, which he washed down with a glass of dark rum.

On the field he remained highly competitive but his captains, Stuart Sutcliffe and Rodney Warhurst, recall few problems with team-mates, opponents or spectators, the only exception coming in his benefit match when Bert Eccles took a catch with the batsman on 48 and was berated by Gilchrist for not letting him reach 50 and earn a collection. It would have meant free drinks for all.

He liked his wicketkeeper, Warhurst or John Murray, to stand back so as to convince batsmen he was bowling faster than he was. If he thought a batsman was dominating, he extended his run to start from the boundary. Although his days of regularly dismissing the whole side were history, he was consistently good for five or six wickets per innings, which helped him to 100 wickets in his first season. His tally, however, paled in comparison to his old rival, Sonny Ramadhin, the professional at Delph and Dobcross, who took 134 wickets in the Saddleworth League championship side in 1976.

Ramadhin had overcome the loss of his parents, aged two, to become the first man of Indian origin to play for West Indies. A mystery spinner who could turn the ball both ways, he mesmerised batsmen until he was overbowled during an epic partnership between Peter May and Colin Cowdrey at Edgbaston in 1957, after which he lost much of his mystique, a development Gilchrist welcomed, since he thought his reputation overblown, especially in comparison to his fellow spinner Valentine.

A quiet, dignified person, Ramadhin wasn't a natural soulmate of Gilchrist's and their relationship descended into acrimony because the former was part of the tour committee that sent the latter home from India.

Ramadhin, like Gilchrist, settled in England and played league cricket and an added tension was apparent whenever they faced each other. Although Gilchrist was doubly keen to come out on top, he rarely did. In the North Staffordshire and District

League in 1961, Ramadhin, the professional at Ashcombe Park, defied him with an undefeated 20 to guide his side to a narrow two-wicket victory, an occasion when he needled Gilchrist with some well-chosen words.

They clashed again when Gilchrist played for Delph as a deputy professional in the Tanner Cup, the Saddleworth League 40-over knockout competition, against Chadwick, who had Ramadhin as their professional. Delph lost a low-scoring match by one wicket with the last pair putting on 20-odd runs as Gilchrist insisted the wicketkeeper and slips go back to near the boundary. According to Delph player Gordon Wood, he wasn't best pleased and stormed off. He later turned up at Delph on Whit Monday, claiming the money he felt he was owed.

The rivalry was still there in 1977 when Greenfield played Delph, the village where Ramadhin ran the White Lion pub for many years. Gilchrist was one of Ramadhin's five wickets, caught for 0, in their total of 134 and although he bowled respectably, he couldn't prevent Delph from winning by four wickets.

That following year Gilchrist encountered umpire Gordon Ripley for the first time. Ripley later wrote: 'I was young and an inexperienced umpire and nervous about coming across such an infamous character for the first time … The rain had poured down all morning and I can't recall if there were any covers – but I doubt it – and the pitch had rolled out with a set sheet across it. The match would probably not have been played in 2020.'

Gilchrist bowled at his end. 'Of course, I kept a close eye on his feet and on one particular ball it was very clear to me that his front foot was going to land well over the popping crease and be a no-ball. I called it. The ball was played out into the covers and I wandered round square of the stumps to be in position for any possible run out, looked down all the creases and to my horror saw a fresh spike mark about three inches behind the popping crease but outside the return crease – it had not been a no ball! What Roy had done was to splay his left foot out to the left at the last second and opened up his body. [It may have been the one he threw!] His front foot had landed quite legitimately behind the popping crease.

'Roy came back and took a long look at the spike mark, he then took a long look at me, he repeated this twice and then said, "You – white honky. You don't know the laws." He would, of course, be in line for a long suspension these days but I simply said, "Roy, I do know the laws and I got that one wrong – sorry!" His skipper walked in from mid-off and said to me, "What's to do, Gordon?" I replied, "I got that no-ball call wrong." He turned to Roy and said, "Forget it, Gilly, get on with the game." We did, but Gilly was still incandescent.

'Later in the innings there was a big appeal for a run-out at the opposite end. Unfortunately, my colleague was standing much too far away (40 yards at least) and he turned the appeal down. Gilly called across to him, "How can you give that decision, you can't see that far!"'

During his time at Greenfield, Ripley saw Gilchrist play in a benefit match for a local XI against a Yorkshire XI at Delph. Geoffrey Boycott opened the innings and Gilchrist, opening the bowling, rolled back the years to go off his full run and bowled three or four overs of genuine pace. 'I'd like to say that he got Boycott out, but I remember correctly it was Boycott caught Sullivan (Lancashire) bowled Ramadhin 37.'

According to Greenfield team-mate Steven Barron, Gilchrist could still bowl very fast, especially against the opposition's best player. 'I remember the hype when he bowled at Bob Zadow, the pro from Flowery Field who was a great batsman. There was a huge crowd who came to see Bob knock Roy all around the ground. Well, Roy pushed himself off the clubhouse wall and sent down a rocket which uprooted Bob's middle stump.'

At the end of that season, Gilchrist contacted his new-ball partner at Crompton, Peter Sutcliffe, about giving him a job, since he was out of work. Out of respect for the man, Sutcliffe, who owned a thermal insulation and sheet-metalwork contracting business, employed him as a full-time driver and found him to be an excellent worker. In return, he persuaded him to join him at Heyside, one of the original members of the Saddleworth League. He agreed immediately and, playing as an amateur, enjoyed considerable success with the club. 'He was, as at Crompton, always at the club during the week at practice nights, supporting it,' recollected Sutcliffe, 'and even arranged for a "quickie" from Montserrat, named Kevin Duberry, to join the club. This was a tremendous success, as Kevin was quick!'

Revered by his team-mates, Gilchrist bowled his leg-cutters with pinpoint accuracy off eight paces, sometimes with an eight-one field, since few batsmen at that level could drive him.

Although competitive enough still to express indignation when a catch went down off his bowling or when taken off, he mellowed with age. One of his first games for his new club was against Stalybridge on a freezing day in April. Heyside fielded first and he bowled 23 overs at Gordon Ripley's end. 'I gave him a few decisions and turned a number of appeals down,' recalled Ripley. 'At the end of the match, as we trudged off, Gilly came up to me, put his arm around my shoulders and said, "You not so bad after all, man." I never had a problem with Roy again; in fact, I like to think we hit it off quite well – I liked him.

'I have been watching bowlers' front feet for 45 seasons now and I have never seen a bowler use the crease in such a way as Gilly. He delivered every ball from a different place and instead of there being two potholes where his foot landed (like other bowlers) there was a three-foot-wide scar along the bowling crease where his right foot had landed. It must have been quite difficult for the batsman with these subtle variations. It was one of them that caught me out when we first met.'

Another memory of Gilchrist comes from Jeremy Scholes, scorer for Flowery Field at this time. He remembered Gilchrist playing for Heyside on a day when he wasn't well. Every over he fielded down by the scorebox coughing and spluttering; looking as if he was about to collapse, 'but he kept going over after over – not at his best but what an indefatigable display and a true commitment to cricket from a great player.'

In 1980 he was the leading wicket-taker in the league, every wicket still a source of satisfaction. During the England–West Indies Test at Old Trafford, Gilchrist turned up to watch some of the match on the Friday and when he was leaving the West Indian dressing room, he said he couldn't make it the next day as he had a game, but would be back on the Monday.

Shortly before tea on the following day, he was spotted. 'What happened, Gilly?' asked one of the team. 'We thought you had a game?'

'Yes, but that finished long time ago,' replied Gilchrist. 'I got five wickets, the rest are in hospital and we just knock off the little runs.'

His one disappointment that year was his failure to shine in the final of the Tanner Cup when Heyside were comprehensively beaten by underdogs Stalybridge.

In 1981 he was back in the news when playing for Heyside against Great Eccleston in the Samuel Whitbread Village Championship, in clear breach of the rules that stated that any first-class cricketer below the age of 60 was ineligible to play. The secretary of Great Eccleston rang up Ben Brocklehurst, the chairman of *The Cricketer*, which organised the competition, to say there was a West Indian down in the scorebook as Carl White who was bowling very fast. Did they know who he was?

When quizzed over Gilchrist's inclusion, Heyside's secretary said, 'I didn't choose the team and anyway I've lost the rules.' By flouting the rules, the club would have been automatically disqualified, but, in the event, it didn't matter because they were bowled out for 50 to lose by some margin.

The next year, in a pre-season friendly against Middleton, he came across Jim Carnegie, their prolific opener, for the first time. He wrote, 'I got to know Roy well and have only good things to say about him. At no time, win or lose, did I witness him losing control.

'By now, he could no longer rely on sheer pace to get his wickets so he turned to swing and seam. Neither worked for him on this occasion.

'After five or six unproductive overs, Roy muttered something indiscernible, and lengthened his run-up by a good ten paces. This may have been the ruse for the more elderly spectators but now added little extra pace. At the end of the over, Roy took his sweater without any histrionics and let others do what they could.'

He also had a hand in the appointment of the club's new professional, Cebert Glasgow, a Barbadian batsman who first encountered Gilchrist when playing for Royton against Crompton in 1973. The opening batsman had gone to a christening and the captain said, 'Who wants to open?' The young Glasgow put up his hand and got right behind the ball when facing Gilchrist, who came down the pitch and inquired, 'Are you scared, young man?'

Glasgow's innings of 19 felt like 50 and it left a lasting impression on Gilchrist, because one day before the 1983 season he turned up unannounced at Glasgow's house and said, 'Glasgy, I recall you faced me and you played me unlike those older men. There is a job at Thornham and I recommend you.'

Glasgow accepted and with the arrival also of Jim Carnegie from Middleton, the batting was immeasurably strengthened. Now approaching 50, gaunt and bespectacled, Gilchrist could only generate pace through a suspect action, batted number 11 and wouldn't chase much in the field. Nevertheless, his enthusiasm remained undiminished. He still loved to bowl and gave no quarter to the opposition batsmen, one of whom was the future England captain Mike Atherton, then a highly talented 14-year-old playing for Woodhouses. In an early game against East Lancashire Paper Mill, he impressed Carnegie with his astute cricket brain, working out batsmen's strengths and weaknesses. One of his four victims that day included the prize scalp of the UK's last dual cricket-football international, Scotland's Andy Goram.

His regular batch of wickets helped Thornham to unprecedented success, since they finished runners-up to Unsworth and reached the semi-final of the Walkden Cup, the Lancashire and Cheshire League knockout competition, for the first time. According to Carnegie, 'The cup semi-final at Greenmount was the only game when I can recall seeing Roy unhappy. He had good reason to be. It was boiling hot, the wicket looked a belter and we won the toss. Our captain, "Dibble", inexplicably and unilaterally, opted to bowl. Our astonishment turned to total disbelief as Dibble announced that he would not follow the successful formula of opening the bowling with Roy and himself. They would bowl their allotted ten overs each at the end (when the initial hard new ball wouldn't be fit to throw for a dog). Roy frowned but said nothing. Every part of the bowling plan failed but Roy did, inadvertently, provide one moment of comic relief. Fielding at third man, that ball rolled gently to him for what looked certain to be one bye. Roy decided to show his displeasure for events by underarming the ball back to the keeper. One then turned into four as Roy let go too late to make the ball fly in the wrong direction back over his head and over the boundary. Those of us far enough away laughed and Roy joined in. We lost!

Carnegie's abiding memory of Gilchrist that year was the Lancashire and Cheshire League dinner at Old Trafford with Jim Laker and Tom Graveney as guest speakers. As the two passed Thornham's table, they spotted Gilchrist and immediately invited him to join them on the podium. 'Roy was overjoyed. Once on the podium, Tom gave Roy a namecheck and related how uncomfortable he'd felt when facing the Black Flash, adding Roy was very, very quick. He really was. Roy bowed modestly in appreciation and gave us all one last beamer.'

In 1984 Gilchrist moved to Stalybridge to pro for them for the next two years. He performed unerringly well, with one possible exception. Carnegie wrote, 'In August, we went there and Stalybridge posted 225/9 declared from their 45 overs – a huge score in the day before T20s made slogging an art rather than something to be sneered at and when edges carried only so far as slip as opposed to flying to the boundary off timber thicker than my thigh. As we took the field after tea, Gilly beamed at me (this time with a smile rather than a dangerous missile) and asked, "Are you going for them, Jim?" We were and cruised home. Despite disappointing figures of 10-1-77-0, Roy accepted defeat in good grace with no trace of a tantrum and even let me buy him a post-match beer!'

After two years at Stalybridge, Gilchrist returned to Thornham for his final season, still a useful opening bowler with his ability to bowl line and length, not least when playing for Middleton past players against the present ones.

In the second round of the Walkden Cup, played on Sundays, Thornham were drawn against a struggling second division side, Romiley, based in Stockport. With the home side requiring an impossible target in five overs, it began to rain. Highly reluctant to embark on a two-hour round trip to complete the game the next day, as the rules required if they had to go off, Gilchrist spoke for everyone when he politely asked the two young batsmen to consider either conceding or indulging in a contrived run-out. When the batsmen flatly resisted his suggestion, declaring they hadn't had a bat the previous day, Gilchrist's calm response was to tell the captain that he would bowl the next over.

After being clubbed for two consecutive fours, he was moved to ask, 'Boy, do you know who I am?'

The boy clearly didn't. 'You're some old bloke who can't bowl,' he declared prompting anxiety among his team-mates, aware of his propensity to over-step and aim high. In actual fact, Gilchrist merely contented himself by hitting the youngster's off stump with a beautiful leg-cutter, commenting, 'No, boy. I'm some old bloke who has just bowled you out.'

In the semi-final against Longsight, Carnegie recalls the tension of the final over. 'The game culminated in a moment of high drama – Roy was set to face the final ball. The scores were level but we were nine down and they were all out. A dot ball, and the victory was ours. A wicket and it was theirs on a faster run rate. Roy played a textbook forward defensive shot. As the ball passed the edge of the bat, there was a noise, followed by a chorus of appeals. Roy pointed to his sweater. Not out!

'A small crowd of angry opponents circled around Roy. Not for the first time in his career, Roy picked up a stump. This was sufficient for the dissenters to cease dissenting. Action (and possibly reputation) had spoken louder than words. After the game with tongues loosed by a few extra beers and Roy having his usual chauffeur, Cebert Glasgow, he was happy to confirm or modify various tales attributed to him. Against Vinoo Mankad, the Rochdale pro. "Skipper say to me, 'How about it, Roy.' "I looked at Mankad. Towels everywhere. Towels under his cap, towels up his sweater, towels down his trousers. I say to skip, 'Give me three balls.' Third ball he's spittin' teeth."'

When asked if given his time again he'd prefer to come back as a batsman, he was most dismissive. 'No, I hate batsmen,' was his mischievous response.

Despite enjoying home advantage in the final, Thornham lost to Denton by 30 runs in a high-scoring game. Although he bowled tidily, Gilchrist went wicketless, but in his final home game against Denton St Lawrence he rolled back the years to take 3-9 off his ten overs. It was truly the end of an era.

Chapter 12

'Ches, I'm not going back'

IN OCTOBER 1986 Gilchrist returned to Jamaica for the first time in 24 years. The occasion was the Milo Melbourne Festival started by Melbourne club president Tony Becca, the distinguished West Indian cricket writer and broadcaster, as a means of boosting the club's finances which had fallen into debt in the 1970s. The festival not only allowed Jamaica to parade its most talented players, it brought many great players, past and present, to the island.

Delighted to be back in his homeland, Gilchrist, accompanied by his Lancashire girlfriend, enjoyed the hospitality shown to him, reminding him of times past, so much so that he kept extending his stay and, later, when Chester Watson gave him his return ticket, he said, 'Ches, I'm not going back.' Aside from his girlfriend, who'd already returned home, he no longer felt comfortable in England now that his cricket career, the original purpose for him settling there, was winding down. Although supported by a loyal body of friends such as Whit Stennett, Euton Christian and Ed Allen, his life lacked a firm anchor as he became detached from his family, drifted from job to job and was less inclined to keep commitments. According to Allen, 'It was sad to see this bloke we admired going into decline.' At Thornham, his final club, he would go round at the end of a game and cadge a glass of rum. He wanted the club to pay for his motor insurance and relied on local benefactors to help settle his debts.

On 27 January 1987, Gilchrist's life took a turn for the better when he met Maureen Dixon, a self-employed dressmaker, at her mother's home in the rural community of Rose Hill. They soon moved in together and in 1989 a daughter, Jerdine, was born, a much-loved sister to Jerdaine, Maureen's son from a previous relationship. (Gilchrist also had a daughter, Norma, from a previous relationship, with whom he had little contact.) The following year they moved into a home in the Eltham housing scheme, Spanish Town, the former capital of Jamaica, some ten miles west of Kingston, courtesy of Roy Decambre, a successful businessman who'd known Gilchrist from youthful tussles in the nets. Disgusted with his treatment by the cricket authorities in Jamaica, he offered Gilchrist a house or car and Maureen told him to take the house. There they settled into a blissful domestic life, Gilchrist proving a loving partner and father to the children, escorting them to and from school, playing games with them and taking them to the cricket. He also liked to cook for them, although not always with success, since on one occasion he fell asleep and burnt the food.

Decambre also helped Gilchrist get a coaching job at St George's College, a Roman Catholic school in Kingston, renowned primarily for its football. He took his duties seriously and his efforts reaped their reward when the school won the colts' cricket league, their first title for more than 30 years. Sadly, his poor health forced him to give up full-time employment and the most he could rely on thereafter was the occasional day's coaching in the rural areas, organised by Chester Watson. Always at ease with ordinary Jamaicans, Gilchrist established a good rapport with his charges and so highly did they appreciate his bowling tutorials that they would present him with little gifts afterwards.

Watson, his closest confidant outside his family and now living back in Jamaica, noted a marked contrast in Gilchrist on his return. Older and frailer, he became a much more emollient personality, less inclined to drink, argue or bear a grudge. In place of the bombastic showman who loved to recount his cricketing triumphs, especially over those he didn't rate, he now refrained from harking back to his career or comparing it favourably with the modern game. Content to go to the cricket, he sat there quietly, saying little except to compliment those who caught his eye. In 1995 Richard Minott, a single-minded 17-year-old, made his debut for Hanover against Melbourne in the Senior Cup. Disappointed with his innings of 17, he was sulking back in the dressing room when one of his team-mates came in and told him that someone wanted to have a word. Minott wasn't keen on talking but he came out anyway and his team-mate pointed to an old man sitting on a chair, informing him that he was Roy Gilchrist. 'I walked over and Mr Gilchrist extended his hand,' recalled Minott. 'I shook his hand and he smiled. We chatted for a little while and he said he liked my determination and courage. He told me that if I continued like this, I would be a successful player, but I needed to work hard on my running between the wickets. I thanked him and walked away with an even greater determination to be a cricket professional.'

Another cricketer to encounter Gilchrist on occasions at Melbourne was Winston Tai, who received a signed copy of his autobiography. He recalled a soft-spoken gentleman who showed no signs of his tempestuous past.

Gilchrist spent much time at Sabina Park, but despite his mellowing with age he remained a pariah to many of the class-conscious cricket establishment, so he wouldn't be given a complimentary pass for big-match occasions. It needed the intervention of Chester Watson to get him a special invite to the Jamaica Cricket Board directors' box, where he proved to be good company. According to Jackie Hendriks, he looked very quiet and shy with no indication of past turmoil.

Along with ill health, Gilchrist's final years were bedevilled by financial hardship. In 1995 he was the recipient of a generous gesture by the recently formed Mound Mania Ltd, which gave part of the gate receipts at the Mound, an uncovered grassed terrace at the north-east end of Sabina Park transformed into a party area, to past cricketers. At a presentation ceremony during the Kingston Test between West Indies and Australia in the presence of the home team, led by captain Richie Richardson, who praised his past service to West Indian cricket, Gilchrist walked away with $50,000, the equivalent of some £1,500. Grateful for such generosity, he said it came at an opportune time, since he was now unemployed. 'Though small in today's high cost of living I will put the sum to good use.'

For some time, Gilchrist had been afflicted by high blood pressure and Parkinson's disease. His doctors told him to stop smoking but he ignored their advice. In time he began to lose a lot of weight and also suffer from Alzheimer's disease. Friends suggested that he return to England to get treatment on the National Health Service, but he wouldn't hear of it. He didn't want to leave Maureen and the family, but with only his disability pension to sustain them money was tight. On his frequent visits to Sabina Park, former West Indies opener and leading cricket administrator Allan Rae used to take pity on him and give him a few dollars.

On England's tour to the West Indies in early 1998 when they were practising at the Kensington Club in Kingston, coach David Lloyd recalled looking out of the pavilion window and seeing this frail little man. 'You don't remember me,' he said. 'I do,' replied Lloyd. 'You are Roy Gilchrist,' and they had a lovely chat. Gilchrist also met up with England manager Bob Bennett, his former captain at Bacup, who was shocked by his physical decline, and captain Mike Atherton, who couldn't believe that this was the same person whose bowling had so terrified him some 15 years earlier.

At the same time, Euton Christian and Whit Stennett, on a trip to Jamaica, had a reunion with Gilchrist, but Gilchrist, all skin and bone and unable to hold a glass, initially didn't recognise them or recall life in Manchester. He also failed to recollect Pankaj Roy scoring two centuries against him in the famous Ranji Trophy match between Bengal and Hyderabad in 1963 when he met the Indian sport journalist Gautam Bhattacharya.

Despite the tender care given to him by Maureen, Gilchrist's health continued to deteriorate and he died at home on 18 July 2001 after a long battle with hypertension and Parkinson's. In the various obituaries of Gilchrist's life, writers not surprisingly recalled his fearsome speed and the fiery temperament that brought a premature end to his international career. *The Times* wrote that Gilchrist was the architect of his own decline, but suggested that his talents could have been better served by more careful handling; David Frith in *The Independent* declared that out of all the fast bowlers to emerge from the Caribbean region, none inflicted more fear into the hearts of batsmen, because of his willingness to bowl beamers; the Trinidad cricket writer B.C. Pires in *The Guardian* reckoned that no one before Gilchrist was more aggressive or faster, and few after him – perhaps Malcolm Marshall, Michael Holding and Colin Croft – displayed his combination of sustained speed and hostility.

Tony Becca in the *Sunday Gleaner* wrote that Gilchrist wasn't blessed with a long career. 'Such was his impact, however, that he must be numbered in the company of the greats.

'He was fast. A little man with exceptionally long arms, he was at his fastest, the fastest West Indian bowler of all time, and probably the fastest bowler the world has ever seen.

'Because his career was short, he may not be among the world's greatest fast bowlers. It is, however, an unforgettable part of West Indies cricket. Such was his speed, such was his impact that he was a legend in his time.'

On 5 August 130 mourners attended his funeral at Dovecote Memorial Park Crematorium, including Tony Becca, Allan Rae, Jackie Hendriks and Chester Watson, who besides writing the eulogy, organised the occasion, inviting the broadcaster Ian Andrews to sing a ballad and Wes Hall to give the address. Hall, an ordained Pentecostal minister and newly appointed president of the WICBC, hailed Gilchrist as the best friend he'd ever had, adding that he was a fallen hero.

'Gilly like Jesus Christ was rejected and rejection is the deepest wound of the soul. I loved Gilly and I knew him as Jesus loved Lazarus. The world knew Gilly for what they read. As long as he had a ball in his hand, he was king.

'In the past they always reminded him as they reminded me – that he was from the proletariat. They would even tell him that he was not a scholar. But he was a quiet person, and I should know, having been his only room-mate for 13 Test matches.'

While accepting that Gilchrist could be difficult, Hall declared he could have been better managed. 'I bear no malice for Alexander and the late Berkeley Gaskin for sending Gilly home and banishing him from Test cricket at the age of 25 [sic]. But there should have been a rehabilitation process and I promise that there will be a rehabilitation process in place now to deal with such matters.'

Although Hall's emotional eulogy understandably touched on the great controversies of former times, it wasn't the whole story. The aggressive spark that had driven Gilchrist to self-destruction gradually burned itself out and he returned to Jamaica to live out his final years a humbler, more complete person, a genial presence to all those he encountered. The one constant theme of his life, his love of cricket, remained, but it was a game no longer beset by intimidation and gamesmanship, rather one of competing skills played essentially for pleasure.

Although increasingly afflicted by ill health and penury, he didn't bemoan his lot, but found contentment in a family he loved and who loved him in turn, so much so that 21 years after his passing, Maureen remarked, 'Gilly was a very kind person and always looked out for his kids. My time with him was joyful and when he died it was a great loss to us.'

Roy Gilchrist

ROY GILCHRIST was a flashing meteor that briefly lit up
the firmament of international cricket in the late 1950s before
crashing to earth in a blaze of acrimony. Small and stocky with
great strength of shoulder, his galloping run-up and high-
arm action proved an awesome sight when bowling flat out.
Gary Sobers rated him the fastest bowler he ever faced, Jackie
Hendriks called him the quickest he ever kept to, and Colin
Cowdrey described him as a brutal bowler with a terrifying yorker
and bouncer. Inflicting as much pain as possible on batsmen,
he exuded menace at every stage and such was his fearsome
reputation that he dismissed many a batsman even before they
reached the middle.

After a remarkably swift rise from obscurity to Test cricket,
Gilchrist learned much from his first series in England in 1957
before unleashing thunderbolts against Pakistan in the Caribbean
months later. His relentless assault so unnerved their leading
batsman, Hanif Mohammad, that he was moved down the order,
but even then, there was little relief from the barrage of bouncers.
He later admitted that facing Gilchrist was often a terrifying
proposition that gave him nightmares thereafter.

His predatory instincts were enhanced when Wes Hall became
his opening partner in India in 1958/59, since they hunted their

prey with a ruthless efficiency that left no means of escape. Yet for all the sharp words, the terrifying speed and broken bones, Gilchrist was more than a mere tearaway. Possessing a sound cricketing brain, his experience of English green tops taught him to vary his speed and substitute raw pace for swing and seam, such as in his match-winning performance against India in the third Test at Calcutta. Given his age and fitness and with Hall at the other end, there is no reason to doubt that had the fates been kinder to him, he could well have gone down in history as one of the game's greatest fast bowlers.

Inevitably any appraisal of Gilchrist's career must focus on the events in India that saw him sent home in disgrace and effectively banished from Test cricket thereafter, a bitter blow to a proud man and something he resented for many years. 'When Gilly was sent home, he was the greatest bowler in the world, but you never heard about him after that,' commented Hall. 'No day is sacrosanct, and you have to understand that as famous as you are, it only takes one silly thing to ruin everything.'

Contrary to what has often been written, Gilchrist's premature return from India wasn't simply the result of him bowling beamers in the match against North Zone, but rather the final act in a whole litany of misdemeanours. Although his temperamental character is attributed to his deprived background in Jamaica, it should be noted that there is little evidence of a disaffected youth during his formative years. Captivated by the game of cricket which he played at every opportunity, Gilchrist's life on the sugar plantation seems by his own admission to have been a happy one and even when he first emerged as a hostile fast bowler, he kept his aggression within acceptable bounds. According to his sponsor and employer Bill Stewart, he never found Gilchrist any trouble, although he later admitted that his meteoric rise on the cricket field had unbalanced him, prompting a deterioration in his conduct. Now playing for higher stakes and increasingly conscious of alien forces such as class and colour, Gilchrist developed a truculent streak which brought him into conflict with authority. According to the WICBC, there were numerous incidents of his egregious behaviour in England in 1957, which cost him half of his tour bonus, and similar disciplinary lapses in the home series against Pakistan, the most serious of which occurred at the team's hotel in Trinidad. The exact nature of his transgression has never been revealed, but it was deemed serious enough to warrant the intervention of the WICBC president and secretary in peace talks with the Queen's Park Hotel management to stave off a public embarrassment. Consequently, Gilchrist departed to India a marked man in the eyes of the board, very much on his final warning.

Despite his sterling efforts on the field and constant success in India, he endured a fractious relationship throughout the tour, not only with captain Gerry Alexander, but also with vice-captain John Holt, a fellow Jamaican like Alexander, and with senior professional Sonny Ramadhin. His rift with the well-to-do Alexander is invariably explained as a clash of social opposites, but while there is undoubtedly truth in this interpretation it wasn't the whole truth. For not only had Gilchrist liked and respected the patrician John Goddard, his captain in England in 1957, his breach with Alexander, a disciplinarian unlike his predecessor, placed him out on a limb from the rest of his team-mates.

What seems to have exacerbated Gilchrist's relationship with Alexander was his constant challenge to his authority, most notably his flouncing out of the team practice before the second Test at Kanpur and his verbal abuse of his captain when he appeared before the tour committee thereafter. Fortunate not to be sent home there and then, he continued to live dangerously, so that by the time of the final game at Amritsar his relationship with Alexander had all but broken down.

In a game such as cricket where the laws about intimidatory bowling are ambiguous and difficult to police, Gilchrist wasn't the first or the last fast bowler to be censured for excessive use of the bouncer. Gregory and McDonald; Larwood and Voce; Lindwall and Miller; Hall and Griffith and Lillee and Thomson were all subjected to critical scrutiny, not to mention the West Indies pace quartet of the 1980s.

The beamer was a different matter. While Gilchrist was technically correct in stating that the ball wasn't illegal (although it was when he threw), it was a lethal delivery when bowled at speed and one that fully contravened the spirit of the game, a fact accepted by every other Test player. Given the frequency with which he employed it and the lack of protective clothing in those days, it was a near miracle that no one was seriously or fatally injured. Other bowlers may well have served up the occasional beamer in frustration, but mainly it was accidental and followed by an immediate apology. In light of a warning by his captain Alexander after the first Test in India to restrict the use of the bouncer and desist from bowling beamers, it was foolhardy of Gilchrist to ignore his orders by resorting to such deliveries against Swaranjit Singh, a friend of his captain, in a relatively minor match at the end of the tour.

Given his past record of misconduct, and his fraught relationship with Alexander, who'd been appointed to restore discipline, Gilchrist could hardly complain about his banishment from India, a fact accepted by most West Indian cricket journalists. According to Michael Manley, 'This was a difficult young man, full of aggression, difficult to handle, burdened with those tensions which so often run like scars across the landscape of the personalities of people who come from poverty.'

With Alexander still captain in the 1959/60 series against England, Gilchrist's omission was understandable, but once his mentor Frank Worrell took over thereafter, the case for his rehabilitation seemed a valid one, especially given Worrell's desire to have him in Australia in 1960/61. It is true that Gilchrist didn't help his cause by giving several uncompromising interviews in which he offered little contrition for past follies and defended his right to bowl beamers, but whatever the nature of his capricious personality, the WICBC refused to engage with him. They rejected C.L.R. James's constructive attempts at mediation and made no allowances for his deprived upbringing. One of the salient points about Gilchrist's life is that, for all his rebellious tendencies, he gave his all to those who took an interest in him: Bill Stewart, his employer and sponsor in Jamaica, Worrell and Fred Mitchell, his captain at Bacup, to name but three. Had he been taken to Australia under Worrell and participated in that most chivalrous of series it is difficult to believe that he would have gone out of his way to let down his captain and good friend by resorting to crude gamesmanship.

No sooner was he given a lifeline by returning to the West Indies to participate in trials for the series against India in 1962, than he was immediately discarded following his life ban by the North Staffordshire League for ungentlemanly conduct. From contemporary reports, Gilchrist clearly acted in a petulant manner in the matches concerned, and his own defence, recorded in his autobiography, isn't entirely convincing. At the same time, the provocation that he had been subjected to that season from the crowds, not least the occasional racist comment, and his inability to put his case either to the North Staffordshire League committee or the WICBC suggest there were mitigating factors that the latter should have taken into account before closing the door for good on his international career.

Cast into oblivion and embittered by his treatment, Gilchrist's festering resentment continued to erupt intermittently on the field. He was by no means the sole instigator of some of these clashes, but aside from the occasions when he lashed out physically, such as against the Australian Lou Laza, there were times when his judgement was seriously awry. Giving one's all in a competitive league match was one thing; bowling bouncers at a 16-year-old in a friendly or scattering the Bishop of Burnley's stumps first ball in a charity match was quite another.

Although Gilchrist's character off the field stood in marked contrast with the angry young man on it, he could still fall prey to his demons when things didn't go his way. Having subjected his wife to many a tribulation in their marriage, his conviction for brutally assaulting her in 1967 was followed by his fight at a cricket match the following year which led to serious assault charges and a custodial sentence. Although prison did nothing to ameliorate the strains in his marriage and the excesses of his profligate lifestyle, he became more restrained on the cricket field. No longer the force of old as rampaging youth gave way to sedate middle age, he swapped extreme pace for military medium and won the allegiance of his younger team-mates by virtue of his continued prowess, allied to his benign paternalism.

Returning to Jamaica in 1986 to live out his final years, he found peace and contentment in his new family and a fresh outlook which consigned his troubled past to history. Yet, sadly, that homecoming was blighted by poverty and ill health, a tragic end in many ways to a turbulent life. Whether one sees Gilchrist as a victim of a rigid hierarchy that wrote him off prematurely, or as the author of his own misfortunes – the writer Peter Oborne called him one of the nastiest pieces of work to stroll on to a cricket field – he placed his own unmistakable stamp on the game. With his belligerent fast bowling and combative personality, he not only helped restore the West Indies' proud tradition of raw pace, a tradition which reached its apogee in the 1970s and 80s, he also challenged the Victorian ethos of cricket as the most genteel of games by terrifying batsmen and electrifying spectators the world over, leaving them with memories they would never forget.

Bibliography

Akeroyd, Paul, *Answering the Call: The Extraordinary Life of Sir Wesley Hall* (Epsom: J.W. McKenzie Ltd, 2022).

Alley, Bill, *My Incredible Innings* (London: Pelham Books, 1969).

Alley, Bill, *Standing the Test of Time* (Manchester: Empire, 1999).

Barker, J.S. and Sobers, Gary, *Cricket in the Sun* (London: Barker, 1967).

Beckles, Hilary, *Liberation Cricket: West Indies Cricket Culture* (Manchester: Manchester University Press, 1995).

Beckles, Hilary, *The Development of West Indies Cricket* (Kingston: UWI Press, 1998).

Benaud, Richie, *Anything But: An Autobiography* (London: Hodder & Stoughton, 1998).

Birbalsingh, Frank with Seecharan, Clem, *Indo-West Indian Cricket* (Hertford: Hansib Publications Ltd, 1996).

Birbalsingh, Frank, *The Rise of West Indian Cricket: From Colony to Nation* (Hertford: Hansib Publications Ltd, 1996).

Carnegie, Jim, *In a Different League: Cricket's North-South Divide* (Market Harborough: Matador, 2009).

Cantrell, John, *Farokh Engineer from the Pavilion End* (Stroud: The History Press, 2004).

Carrington, Ben and McDonald, Ian, *'Race', Sport and British Society* (London: Routledge, 2001).

Cleary John, *A Class Innings* (self-published, 2009).

Cowdrey, Colin, *MCC: The Autobiography of a Cricketer* (London: Hodder & Stoughton, 1976).

Cowdrey, Colin, *The Incomparable Game* (London: Hodder & Stoughton, 1970).

Cozier, Tony, *Sir Everton Weekes: An Appreciation* (Epsom: J.W. McKenzie Books, 2017).

D'Oliveira, Basil, *Time to Declare* (London: J.M. Dent, 1980).

Dolman, Steve, *Edwin Smith: A Life in Derbyshire Cricket* (Cardiff: ACS, 2015).

Evans, Colin, *Farokh Engineer: The Cricketing Cavalier* (Nantwich: Max Books, 2017).

Fazal Mahmood, *From Dust to Dawn: Autobiography of a Cricket Legend* (Oxford: OUP, 2003).

Farnworth, Chris and Hall, Stanley, *Bacup CC: The Authorised History* (Burnley Print, 2000).

Goodwin, Clayton, *Caribbean Cricketers from the Pioneers to Packer* (London: Harrap, 1980).

Guha, Ramachandra, *Wickets in the East* (Oxford, OUP India,1992).

Hall, Wes, *Pace like Fire* (London: Pelham Books, 1965).

Hanif Mohammad, *Playing for Pakistan: An Autobiography* (Karachi: Hamdard Press, 1999).

Heywood, Freda, Malcolm and Brian, *In a League of their Own: Cricket and Leisure in 20th Century Todmorden* (Todmorden: Upper Calder Publications, 2011).

Hignell, Andrew, *Jack Mercer* (Cardiff: ACS, 2011).

Kanhai, Rohan, *Blasting for Runs* (London: Souvenir Press, 1966).

Kardar, Abdul Hafeez, *Green Shadows* (Karachi: self-published, 1958).

Kay, John, *Cricket in the Leagues* (London: Eyre & Spottiswoode, 1970).

James, C.L.R., *Beyond a Boundary* (London: Stanley Paul, 1963).

Laker, Jim, *Over to Me* (London: Frederick Muller Ltd, 1960).

Lawrence, Bridgette, *Masterclass: The Biography of George Headley* (Leicester: Polar, 1995).

Lewis, Vic, *Music and Maiden Overs: My Showbusiness Life* (London: Chatto & Windus, 1987).

Manley, Michael, *A History of West Indies Cricket* (London: Andre Deutsch, 1987).

May, Peter, *A Game Enjoyed* (London: Stanley Paul, 1985).

Murtagh, Andrew, *Test of Character*: *The Story of John Holder – Fast Bowler and Test Match Umpire* (Worthing: Pitch Publishing, 2014).

Oborne, Peter, *Wounded Tiger: A History of Cricket in Pakistan* (London: Simon & Schuster, 2014).

Pearson, Harry, *Slipless in Settle: A Slow Turn Around Northern Cricket* (London, Little, Brown, 2012).

Piesse, Ken, *Pep: The Story of Cec Pepper* (Mount Eliza, Victoria, Cricket Books.Com Au, 2018).

Ross, Alan, *Through the Caribbean* (London: Hamish Hamilton, 1960).

Rowe, Mark, *The Summer Field: A History of English Cricket since 1840* (Cardiff: ACS, 2016).

Sandford, *Christopher, Godfrey Evans: A Biography* (London: Simon & Schuster, 1990).

Seecharan, Clem with McDonald, Ian, *Joe Solomon and the Spirit of Port Mourant* (Hertford: Hansib Publications Ltd, 2022).

Sissons, Ric and Stoddart, Brian, *Cricket and the Empire* (London: Allan & Unwin, 1984).

Sobers, Gary, *My Autobiography* (London: Headline, 2002).

Sobers, Gary, *Twenty Years at the Top* (London: Pan Books 1989).

Stennett, Whit, *A Bitter Sweet Journey* (Manchester: The Basford Press, 2007).

Stollmeyer, Jeff, *Everything Under the Sun* (London: Stanley Paul, 1983).

Wadhwaney, K.R., *Indian Cricket Controversies* (New Delhi: Diamond Pocket Books Ltd, 2017).

Walcott, Clyde, *Island Cricketers* (London: Hodder and Stoughton, 1958).

Walcott, Clyde, *60 Years on the Back Foot* (London: Victor Gollancz, 1999).

Wilkinson, Geoff, A *Century of Bradford League Cricket* (The Bradford League, 2003).

Wild, Noel, *The Greatest Show on Turf* (Nelson: Hendon Publishing Company Ltd, 1992).

Worrell, Frank, *Cricket Punch* (London: Stanley Paul, 1959).

Woodhouse, David, *Who Only Cricket Knows: Hutton's Men in the West Indies 1953/54* (Bath: Fairfield Books, 2021).

Newspapers and periodicals

Barbados Advocate, Bacup Times, Birmingham Post, Bolton News, Burnley Express, Caribbean Quarterly, Civil and Military Gazette (Lahore), *Cricketer, Crewe Chronicle, Daily Argosy, Daily Chronicle* (British Guiana), *Daily Gleaner, Daily Herald, Daily Mail, Daily Mirror, Daily Telegraph, Daily Telegraph* (India), *Guardian, Heywood Advertiser, Hindustan Times, Hindu, Independent, Jamaica Observer, Lancashire Evening Telegraph, Manchester Evening News, Middleton Guardian, Nantwich Chronicle, Nation* (Barbados), *Nation* (Trinidad), *Oldham Chronicle, People, Playfair Cricket Monthly, Public Opinion, Sentinel, Star* (Jamaica). *Stone Guardian, Sunday Chronicle* (British Guiana), *Sunday Times, Times, Times of India, Trinidad Guardian, Wisden Cricket Monthly.*

Online Resources

BBC News Online
Cricket Archive – cricketarchive.com
ESPN cricket info – www.espncricketinfo.com
Kaiteur News – www.kaiteurnewsonline.com
Lancashire League – www.lancashireleague.com
Madras Musings – www.madrasmusings.com
Stabroek News – www.stabroeknews.com
Wikipedia-en.wikipedia.org

Index

Abbot, John, 174
Abrahams, Cec, 188
Achong, Ellis, 89
Acton, Bob, 102
Adcock, Neil, 98
Adhikari, Hemu, 77, 151
Akeroyd, Paul, 46
Alexander, Gerry, 7, 9, 10, 34, 38, 44,
    48, 50-6, 61, 64-5, 67-73, 76, 78-87,
    124-8, 132-4, 140, 180, 208, 211-13
Alli-Shaw, M.S., 138
Allen, Ed, 25, 166, 180-1, 202
Alley, Bill, 42-3
Amarnath, Lala, 78, 127
Anderson, Jack, 48, 60, 64, 128
Armstrong, Warwick, 13
Atherton, Mike, 198, 206
Atkins, A.G., 124
Atkinson, Denis, 36, 46
Atkinson, Eric, 63, 77
Austin, Tom, 166
Australian Board of Control, 13, 116
Bailey, Malcolm, 119
Bailey, Trevor, 40-1, 45
Bamber, John, 190
Barber, Len, 118, 121
Barker, J. S., 55-6
Barlow, Alf, 90, 94–95
Barlow, Eddie, 91, 157
Barlow, S.S., 105
Barnes, S.F, 109, 116
Barron, Steven, 194
Bartels, Bob, 98
Batby, James, 104
Batley, Ian, 103
Becca, Tony, 202, 207

Benaud, Richie, 52, 167
Bennett, Bob, 143, 145, 206
Berry, Alan, 190
Bertram, Arnold, 19
Bhandarkar, Kamal, 77
Bhattacharya, Gautam, 206
Bhattacharya, Gopal, 152,
Bickley, Derek, 173-4
Binns, Alfie, 33
Blackhurst, Malcolm, 143
Blake, David, 34
Board of Control for Cricket in India,
    78, 146-7, 153
Boardman, Peter, 176
Bolton, Bill, 170
Bonitto, Colin, 28-9
Bonitto, Neville, 28
Booth, David, 103, 105
Borde, Chandu, 65, 76-8, 112, 162
Bose, Mihir, 62
Bowes, Bill, 45
Boycott, Geoff, 194
Bradman, Don, 13-14, 93
Briggs, Albert, 174
Britton, Joseph, 90, 93
Brocklehurst, Ben, 197
Brocklehurst, John, 191
Broomhead, Harry, 103
Bryan, Dora, 102
Bull, Geoff, 117, 168-9
Burnet, Ronnie, 112
Burnett, Harold, 32
Burrowes, Foggy, 30
Bustamante, Alexander, 18
Butcher, Basil, 10, 31, 61, 69, 71, 84,
    144, 158

Cahill, Gerard, 163
Cardus, Neville, 14
Carnegie, Jim, 198-200
Carr, Donald, 41
Carrick, Tommy, 154-5, 162
Chapman, Brian, 37
Chappell, Ian, 170
Chichester, Charles, 125
Chidambaram, M, 146-7, 154
Chisholm, S.A., 104
Christian, Euton, 14, 166, 202, 206
Clarke, Doug, 102, 164, 169, 174
Cleary, John, 161
Close, Brian, 38-40, 185
Columbus, Christopher, 16
Constantine, Learie, 21, 23, 35, 89, 114, 154, 179, 185
Contractor, Nari, 74
Cooper, Ed, 171
Coppin, Seymour, 32, 124, 128, 134, 136, 138
Cortley, John, 174
Cowdrey, Colin, 39-42, 44-5, 49, 131, 192, 209
Cox, Dennis, 117, 119, 168-9
Cozier, Tony, 53
Crawford, Pat, 96
Croft, Colin, 207
Cronkshaw, Jack, 111
Crump, Brian, 116
Dare, John, 139
Davidson, Alan, 52
Davis, (Gilchrist), Lucy, 19
Dawson, Harold, 163
Day, Harvey, 45
Day, Philip Edgar, 184
de Caires, Cecil, 24, 32, 34
Debenham, Chris, 176
Decambre, Roy, 203
Depeiaza, Clairmonte, 33, 159, 169
Derbyshire, Brian, 172
Desai, Ramakant, 61, 77
Dewdney, Tom, 37-8, 95, 107
Dixon, Bill, 174
Dixon, Jerdaine, 203
Dixon, Jerdine, 203
Dixon, Maureen, 203, 205-6, 208
Dodds, Dickie, 38
D'Oliveira, Basil, 108, 114
Donald, Allan, 152

Dunkerley, Mike, 172
Duberry, Kevin, 195
Dyson, Jack, 177
Eastwood, Leslie, 156
Eccles, Bert, 192
Edmundson, Syd, 145
Engineer, Farokh, 73, 148, 150-1
Evans, Colin, 184
Evans, Godfrey, 39-41
Eyre, Edward, John, 17
Fazal Mahmood, 57-9
Fingleton, Jack, 13
Fletcher, S.S., 105
Frain, Geoff, 101
Francis, George, 23
Franklin, Ronnie, 164
Freckleton, Baz, 85
Frith, David, 207
Friend, Ted, 170
Fuller, Dickie, 27
Gaekwad, S.P., 150
Garband, John, 19
Garvey, Marcus, 18-19
Gaskin, Berkeley, 9, 60, 67, 70-3, 80-1, 85-6, 125-6, 138-40, 208
Ghulam Ahmed, 64, 75, 147
Gibbes, Glendon, 31
Gibbes, Michael, 124
Gibbs, Lance, 31, 57, 134
Gilchrist, Andrew, 181
Gilchrist, Charles, 19
Gilchrist, John, 20, 25, 28
Gilchrist, Mark, 181
Gilchrist, Michael, 181
Gichrist, Novlyn, 12, 94, 135, 181-3, 187
Gilchrist, Paul, 181
Gilchrist, Samuel, 20
Gilligan, Harold, 136
Gladwin, Cliff, 47, 116
Glasgow, Cebert, 197-8, 201
Goddard, John, 35, 42, 45, 48-9, 69, 211
Gomez, Gerry, 129, 132, 134
Gordon, Albert, 21
Gordon, Gertrude, 20
Goram, Andy, 198
Goswami, Chuni, 152
Grace, W.G., 13
Graveney, Tom, 34, 40, 42, 44-5, 49, 199
Greenwood, Eric, 96

Greenwood, Ian, 144
Gregory, Jack, 13, 212
Griffith, Charlie, 14, 23, 141, 157, 160, 212
Griffith, Herman, 23
Grimshaw, Terry, 172
Groves, Johnny, 136, 139
Gupte, Subhash, 95, 145
Gurunathan, S.K., 78
Haigh, Alan, 164-5
Hall, Jess, 119
Hall, Wes, 9, 14, 23, 37-8, 43, 46, 61-5, 69, 71-7, 79, 81-3, 108, 134, 141, 144-6, 157, 160-1, 169, 207-9, 212-13
Halley Bernard, 172-3
Halstead, Roger, 172
Hanif Mohammad, 8, 52-9, 90-1, 166, 209
Hanumant Singh, 150
Hardikar, Manohar, 66, 73
Hartley, Wilson, 189
Harvey, Peter, 121
Hassett, Lindsay, 35
Hazare, Vijay, 62
Hayes, Jack, 158
Haynes, Dennis, 117
Headley, George, 14, 21, 37, 89
Heine, Peter, 98
Hendriks, Jackie, 27, 32-3, 51, 72, 82, 85, 133, 205, 207, 209
Heywood, T, 90
Higgs, Ken, 115
Higgin, Brian, 158
Hilton, Malcolm, 161
Hobbs, Jack, 185
Hodson, Arthur, 123
Holden, Tony, 155
Holder, John, 104-5, 110, 189
Holderness, George, 165
Holding, Michael, 23, 191, 207
Holland, George, 93
Holt, John (junior), 74, 77, 81, 211
Horner, Jack, 128
Hunte, Conrad, 53, 59, 61, 69, 72, 81, 87, 89, 112, 137, 140
Hutton, Len, 36, 185
Hyde, Jimmy, 92, 95, 103-4
Hylton, Leslie, 23, 181
Ikin, Jack, 115
Ikram Elahi, 154
Illingworth, Ray, 185
Imtiaz Ahmed, 53-4, 57
Ince, Carl, 178
Jaisimha, M.L., 152-3
Jamaica Cricket Board, 10-11, 21, 24, 129-130, 135-7, 139-40, 205
James, C.L.R., 10-11, 19, 28, 47, 52, 129, 132-3, 213
Jardine, Douglas, 13
Jayasinghe, Stanley, 162-3
John, George, 23
Jonas, Pryor, 58
Jones, Alan, 189
Jones, Neil, 184
Jowett, Malcolm, 154
Kanhai, Rohan, 31, 35, 57, 61, 67, 69, 81, 84, 165, 169
Kardar, A.H., 58-9
Kay, John, 96, 166
Kenny, Ramnath, 149
Kimber, Jack, 103
King, Frank, 44
King, Lester, 23, 137, 146, 153
Kripal Singh, 76
Krishnaswamy, A.S., 75
Kuckreja, S.N., 74
Laker, Jim, 43-4, 194
Lancaster, Thomas, 157
Lansdale, Alan, 177
Larwood, Harold, 78, 212
Lashley, Peter, 116-17
Lawton, Bill, 93, 102-5
Laza, Lou, 11, 169-70, 214
Leach, Ken, 99
Lee, Brett, 152
Lee, Francis, 176
Lewis, Vic, 168-9
Lillee, Dennis, 15, 212
Lindo, Vince, 31, 179-80
Lindwall, Ray, 13-15, 98, 156, 212
Lloyd, Clive, 52
Lloyd, David, 158, 206
Loader, Peter, 43, 45
Longbottom, Donald, 161
Lord, Mary, 108
Lord, Bob, 156-8
Lord, Cyril, 115
Lowe, Jack, 173
Lymbery, Brian, 185-7

MacLeod, Doug, 117
Madray, Ivan, 58, 67-8
Mahmood Hussain, 56
Manjrekar, Vijay, 74, 77-8, 95, 150
Mankad, Vinoo, 75-7, 90, 94, 201
Manley, Michael, 18, 54, 87, 213
Manley, Norman, 18
Marley, Cecil, 48, 128
Marsh, Brian, 173
Marshall, Roy, 34, 180
Marshall, Malcolm, 207
Martindale, Manny, 23, 32, 89
Marylebone Cricket Club, 12, 13, 36, 100, 109, 112, 116, 125, 129, 132
May, Peter, 39-40, 42, 44-5, 45, 192
McCormack, Vincent, 136, 139
McDonald, Bill, 173
McDonald, Ted, 13, 110, 212
McGuiness, John, 183
McLeod, Norman, 156
McMorris, Easton, 28, 53
McWatt, Clifford, 33
Meckiff, Ian, 98
Menon, Suresh, 74
Mercer, Jack, 23
Milka Singh, A.G., 148
Miller, Keith, 13-15, 98, 134, 212
Mills, Grenville, 105
Minott, Richard, 204
Mitchell, Fred, 111-13, 143, 145, 213
Mitra, Kalyan, 94
Mitra, Shyam, 149, 152
Mohan, Inder, 149
Molyneux, Frank, 102
Moore, Bill, 107
Moore, Cliff, 111
Morley, Derek, 120-1
Murray, John, 192
Nadkarni, Bapu, 150
Newbolt, Henry, 14
Norfolk, Duke of, 34
Nurse, Seymour, 146, 157
Oborne, Peter, 215
Ogden, David, 100
Orr, Craig, 160
Pairaudeau, Bruce, 31
Palmer, Annie, 26
Palmer, Ken, 43
Peel, Bobby, 109
Peirce, Tom, 37, 48, 50

Pepper, Cec, 90, 93, 95, 108, 157, 170
Phadkar, Dattu, 93-4
Philpott, Peter, 162
Pickup, Jeff, 112
Piesse, Ken, 93
Pires, B.C., 207
Pitt, Charles, 115
Platt, Ken, 119
Pogson, Rex, 92, 95, 106, 114
Prabhu, K.N., 153
Price, Eric, 166
Rae, Allan, 31, 206-7
Raine, David, 121
Ramadhin, Sonny, 33, 35, 39, 49, 51, 68-9, 81, 95, 108, 115-17, 192-4, 211
Ramchand, V.S., 66, 76-7
Ramnarayan, Venkatraman, 148
Ranjane, Vasant, 62
Reid, Hedley, 21
Reid, John, 33-4
Richardson, Peter, 40, 42
Richardson, Richie, 205
Ripley, Gordon, 102, 193-5
Roberts, Strebor, 32-3, 48, 55, 126-7, 136, 138
Rocca, Paul, 106
Rodriguez, Willie, 68, 82, 85
Rorke, Gordon, 98
Ross, Alan, 133
Roy, Ambar, 153
Roy, Pankaj, 66, 70, 152-3
Roy, Pranab, 152
Roydes, Trevor, 91, 103
Rudkin, Bryan, 186
Rutherford, John, 97-8, 167-8
Rutnagur, Dicky, 83
Saeed Ahmed, 56
Salvi, Ramachandra, 62
Sang Hue, Douglas, 140
Sarbadhikari, Beri, 74
Saxena, Umpire, 153
Scarlett, Reg, 168-9, 181
Schofield, Jack, 165
Scholes, Jeremy, 196
Scholfield, John, 122
Scott, Tommy, 128
Sealey, Ben, 32
Shani, Umpire, 152
Sheppard, David, 44
Shodan, Deepak, 62

Simmons, Jack, 163, 165
Simpson, Bobby, 98
Slater, Archie, 157
Slinger, Edward, 112, 163
Smellie, Tom, 23
Smith, Cammie, 137
Smith, Collie, 9, 30, 35, 39, 42, 61, 69,
    77, 89, 95, 107, 179
Smith, Don, 40
Smith, Edwin, 41, 47
Sobers, Gary, 35, 38, 53-4, 57, 59, 61,
    65, 69, 79, 82-3, 85, 89, 107-8, 141,
    168-9, 178, 209
Solomon, Joe, 31, 61, 69, 77
Squire, Leonard, 186
St Hill, Edwin, 185
Statham, Brian, 31, 98
Stayers, Charlie, 138, 146
Steel, Edward, 183
Steele, David, 115
Steele, John, 116, 119
Stennett, Whit, 26-7, 165-6, 180-1,
    202, 206
Stewart, Bill, 8, 20, 27-8, 130-1, 210,
    213
Stewart, Micky, 38
Stollmeyer, Jeffrey, 36, 51
Subbarayan, P. S., 76
Sullivan, John, 194
Sutcliffe, Peter (Crompton), 171, 195
Sutcliffe, Peter (Lowerhouse), 163
Sutcliffe, Stuart, 191
Sutcliffe, Wilf, 91
Surjit Singh Majithia, 78
Swanton, E.W., 38, 129
Swaranjit Singh, 7, 79-80, 212
Tai, Winston, 204
Talbot, Tom, 116
Tayfield, Hugh, 156
Taylor, Bob, 116
Taylor, Frank (Colne), 143
Taylor, Frank, (Crompton), 188
Taylor, Jaswick, 59, 63
Thomas, George, 149
Thomson, Jeff, 15, 212
Thomson, Philip, 32
Thornton, Alf, 110
Tolhurst, Dave, 102, 174
Townshend, Errol, 125-6, 132
Trueman, Fred, 14, 39, 43-4, 156

Turner, Bob, 160
Tyson, Frank, 89, 91, 98
Umrigar, Polly, 64-5, 77, 151
Valentine, Alf, 33, 35, 68, 89, 95, 192
Vanterpool, Tony, 135
Verity, Gerald, 169
Verity, Hedley, 89
Vittal Rao, T.B., 78
Vizianagaram, Maharajkumar of, 146
Voce, Bill, 212
Vodrey, Frank, 116, 122
Wadekar, Ajit, 151
Walcott, Clyde, 22, 31, 33, 35, 46-7, 50,
    54, 61, 89, 163
Wallis Mathias, 58
Walwyn, Murphy, 187
Warburton, Les, 92
Wardle, Johnny, 112-13, 144, 157
Warhurst, Rodney, 191-2
Warner, Pelham, 13
Washbrook, Cyril, 115
Watson, Chester, 19, 20, 23, 89, 123,
    140, 145-7, 164, 181, 202, 204, 207
Watson, Willie, 34
Wazir Mohammad, 56-7
Weekes, Everton, 22, 33, 35, 47-8, 50,
    53, 61, 89, 110, 140, 179
West Indies Cricket Board of Control,
    10-12, 33, 48, 50, 60, 72, 80, 100,
    124-5, 127-132, 134-5, 137-9, 146,
    207, 211, 213-14
Wharton, Alan, 115
Whiston, Don, 119
Whittaker, Alan, 155
Whittle, Mel, 191
Wild, Noel, 95
Wildgoose, Steve, 163
Wilkinson, Kevin, 159
Wilson, Barry, 113, 145
Wishart, Ken, 135
Wood, Gordon, 193
Woodfull, Bill, 13
Woodhouse, Anthony, 185
Worrell, Frank, 10-12, 20, 22, 28, 35-6,
    38, 40-2, 45, 47, 50, 52, 61, 67, 89-
    90, 95, 97, 110, 116, 125, 131-7, 164,
    169, 179, 181, 213
Wright, Cec, 97, 178, 190
Wright, Glaister, 135
Zadow, Bob, 195